Dramatic Play Lists
1591-1963

By CARL J. STRATMAN, C.S.V.

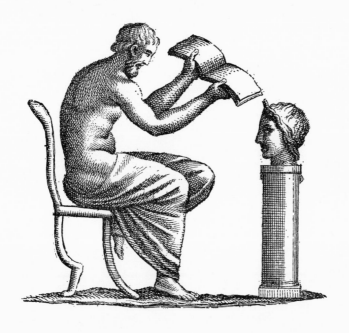

THE NEW YORK PUBLIC LIBRARY

Astor, Lenox and Tilden Foundations

1966

Library of Congress Catalog Card Number: 66–22385

Cover illustration from the *Picture Collection*

Reprinted from the
Bulletin of The New York Public Library
February, March 1966
Printed at The New York Public Library
form p740 [vi-3-66 1m]

W ITH EACH passing year the field of English drama is surveyed more accurately, so that familiarity with its entirety is possible to a greater extent today than even thirty years ago. Among those particularly responsible for the increase in the knowledge of English drama are the numerous scholars who, in one way or another, have contributed to the growth of dramatic bibliography. Scholars such as E. K. Chambers, Allardyce Nicoll, Walter W. Greg, Gerald E. Bentley, Emmett L. Avery, Arthur H. Scouten, George Winchester Stone, Jr., and William Van Lennep, by gathering more accurate information about thousands of plays of the past centuries, have helped to correct numerous errors and to place these works in their proper perspective.

Because the number and variety of dramatic bibliographies continue to multiply, some guide or survey is needed which will enumerate and evaluate for the scholar those works which have poured from the presses during the last three centuries. Although this study does not attempt to provide a guide or survey of the entire field of dramatic bibliography, it is devoted to one of the most important phases, and that is an enumeration and evaluation of those works concerned with actual play titles. Thus, its concern is with printed play lists, whether issued separately or as part of larger works, from 1591, when Philip Henslowe began keeping the famous *Diary* which fur-

[3]

nishes the earliest record of the English theatre, to 1963. The arrangement of the titles which appear in this study is chronological, so as to indicate the gradual growth and development of play lists, to indicate their dependence upon one another — often repeating the errors of their predecessor — and to assess the value of each list.

In short, this study attempts to include every significant work which relates, in some way, to the category of dramatic play lists. As a result, some works are included, even though they are not primarily play lists, because they contain titles of a large number of plays in the form either of dictionaries of actors and actresses, or of general histories which append such lists at the conclusion of the historical section. Briefly the objectives are:

1) To provide a chronological arrangement of those works in which lists of English plays are to be located from the earliest date to 1963.

2) To present the full title of each work, the imprint, and the pagination.

3) To indicate the scope of each work.

4) To give the total number of plays in each work and, whenever possible, the number of authors. (For most of the entries, the only way to arrive at the actual number of plays contained is by counting the individual plays located in the index or, in the absence of an index, by counting the number of plays on each page of the volume. Although the same method is followed in determining the number of authors, it is sometimes impractical to give a total number, especially when the plays are arranged in alphabetical order. For example, when a particular play list contains five thousand or more play titles in alphabetical order, the task of attempting to assemble the works under the names of their various authors becomes most difficult. This study, however, is more concerned with the number of plays than with the number of authors.)

5) To give some indication of the relative merits of the specific work as reference tool.

6) To list the editions of the work, when more than one appear, and to indicate any changes.

7) To note the publication of additions and corrections of specific works, or of scholarly studies devoted to a particular list.

In a study of dramatic play lists, it is important not only to include all works which fall within the scope of such a survey but also to exclude those individual works which, for one reason or another, are not pertinent to the objectives. Thus, the following works and types of works are omitted:

1) Lists which have never been printed, and which exist today only in manuscript form.

2) Lists in booksellers' catalogues after the seventeenth century, as they generally serve to indicate only the plays held by the particular bookseller.

3) Plays listed in auction catalogues of private libraries.

4) Lists of children's plays.

5) Library catalogues, such as those printed for the British Museum, the Library of Congress, and the Bibliothèque Nationale.

6) Histories of theatres or dramatic companies, or of drama in general, which do not contain lists of plays.

7) Collections of play bills as such.

8) The *Short-Title Catalogue* by Pollard and Redgrave, as well as the one by Donald Wing, since neither of these works lists plays in a separate section.

9) The *Dictionary of National Biography*.

10) Bibliographies limited to the writings of a single playwright or group of specific authors.

11) Lists of puppet plays.

12) Guides to "Great Plays."

13) Digests of plays, with plot outlines.

14) Indexes of Monologs and Dialogs.

15) Indexes of Skits and Stunts.

Throughout this study, unless otherwise noted, the term "play" includes not only comedies, tragedies, and farces, but most forms of dramatic entertainment such as moralities, mysteries, miracles, operas, oratorios, masques, triumphs, interludes, drolls, political dialogues, burlettas, divertisements, ballad operas, sketches, burlesques, vaudevilles, and musical entertainment. The word "format" as employed in this study indicates that a particular work specifies whether the printed edition of a play is in folio, quarto, octavo, or duodecimo.

1 *The Diary of Philip Henslowe, from 1591 to 1609.* Printed from the original Manuscript preserved at Dulwich College. Ed by J. Payne Collier . . . London, printed for the Shakespeare Society 1845. xxxiv 290 p

297 plays are mentioned. Although not a list of plays as such, the diary is one of the earliest records which actually gives the titles of plays. The great bulk of the manuscript is in the hand of Philip Henslowe and gives a daily entrance of performances, with breaks from February 19 1592 to November 5 1597. This particular edition contains a number of forged interpolations which are ascribed to Collier. The work is the chief source for theatrical history between 1590 and 1604 and, for this reason, is included here.

For later and better editions see: 1) *Henslowe's Diary.* Ed by Walter W. Greg (London, A. H. Bullen 1904) 2 vols; 2) *Henslowe's Diary.* Ed with supplementary material, introduction and notes by R. A. Foakes and R. T. Rickert (Cambridge, Univ Press 1961) lix [1] 368 p

1656 ROGERS AND LEY CATALOGUE

2 *The Careles Shepherdess.* A Tragi-comedy Acted before the King & Queen, And at Salisbury-Court, with great Applause. Written by T. G. Mr. of Arts. . . . With an Alphabeticall Catalogue of all such Plays that ever were Printed. London, Printed for Richard Rogers and William Ley, and are to be sould at Pauls Chaine nere Doctors commons 1656. 76 p

505 entries for plays. This is the earliest catalogue purporting to give titles of all plays printed to date. The arrangement is alphabetical but under the first letter only. In addition, the earlier works tend to be listed first under each letter. A number of duplications do appear. Occasionally authors' names are appended, sometimes inaccurately. The work

is carelessly printed with the result that there are a number of misprints and other errors. In brief, it is a perfunctory compilation and its main value today is historical. A copy of the list will be found reprinted in W. W. Greg's *A List of Masques* and also in his *A Bibliography Of The English Printed Drama To The Restoration.*

1656 ARCHER'S CATALOGUE

3 *The Excellent Comedy, called The Old Law: Or, A new way to please you. By Phil. Massinger. Tho. Middleton. William Rowley.* Acted before the King and Queene at Salisbury House, and at severall other places, with great Applause. Together with an exact and perfect Catalogue of all the Playes, with the Authors Names, and what are Comedies, Tragedies, Histories, Pastoralls, Masks, Interludes, more exactly Printed than ever before. London, Printed for Edward Archer, at the signe of the Adam and Eve, in Little Britaine 1656. 76 p

The exact title of the catalogue reads: An Exact and perfect Catalogue of all the Plaies that were ever printed; together, with all the Authors names; and what are Comedies, Histories, Interludes, Masks, Pastorals, Tragedies: And all these Plaies you may either have at the Signe of the Adam and Eve, in Little Britain; or, at the Ben Johnson's Head in Thredneedle-street, over against the Exchange.

622 entries for plays. The catalogue is obviously indebted to the work by Rogers and Ley as some of the same errors are perpetuated, and there are 22 apparent cases of repetition. Authors are usually indicated and, for the first time, an attempt is made to indicate the nature of each play. The assignment of authors, however, is often purely arbitrary. Again, the arrangement is alphabetical by letter and, as before, within each letter there is the same tendency to put the early plays first. The value of the work lies in the fact that it has more titles than the former catalogue and that it attempts to designate the type of each play. The catalogue is bibliographically independent.

For the possibility that Pollard compiled the catalogue rather than Archer, see W. W. Greg's *A Bibliography Of The English Printed Drama To The Restoration,* III 1328. Greg's work reprints the list. Further, for the dependence of this work on the Rogers and Ley catalogue, see W. W. Greg, "The Date of the Earliest Play-Catalogues." *The Library,* 5th ser II (Sept – Dec 1947) 190–191.

1661 KIRKMAN'S CATALOGUE

4 [Kirkman, Francis.] *A True, perfect, and exact Catalogue of all the Comedies, Tragedies, Tragi-Comedies, Pastorals, Masques and Interludes, that were ever yet printed and published, till this present year 1661.* all which you may either buy or sell at the several shops of Nath. Brook at the Angel in Cornhil, Francis Kirkman at the John Fletchers Head, on the Back-side of St. Clements, Tho. Johnson at the Golden Key in St. Pauls Churchyard, and Henry Marsh at the Princes Arms in Chancery-lane near Fleetstreet 1661. 16 p

685 plays are listed. Although Kirkman states that the work lists 690 plays, a count reveals 685. He keeps the alphabetical arrangement under the first letter and the tendency of the earlier lists to put earlier plays first in a somewhat haphazard chronological order. There are a number of errors repeated from the earlier lists which Kirkman used, although he does eliminate duplication.

There were two issues of the second impression (1661) of *Tom Tyler and His Wife.* In one, after the title of the play, mention is made of the *Catalogue.* The title is as follows: *Tom Tyler and His Wife. An Excellent Old Play, As It was Printed and Acted about a hundred years ago. Together, with an exact Catalogue of all the playes that were ever yet printed.* The second impression. London: Printed in the year, 1661.

The catalogue is bibliographically independent. The Newberry Library copy has twelve leaves bound with the catalogue, with manuscript additions of 76 plays, giving title and author. A copy of the list of plays will be found reprinted in W. W. Greg's *A Bibliography Of The English Printed Drama To the Restoration.*

[1665?] OXINDEN'S COMMONPLACE BOOK

5 Dawson, G. E. "An Early List of Elizabethan Plays," *Library*, 4th Ser xv (March 1935) 445–456

Dawson reprints the list of 123 plays which are to be found in the manuscript Common-place Book by Henry Oxinden, of Barham, Kent (1608–1670). The manuscript is at the Folger Shakespeare Library in Washington, D.C. Of the 123 titles which Oxinden lists of printed plays, he gives authors' names for thirteen and dates for sixty-two, indicating the first edition in all but eight cases. The list itself is arranged in six different sections, with no apparent attempt at accuracy or consistency. Frequently Oxinden gives the second title for a particular work or an abbreviated form. The dates of the plays listed range from 1565 (*King Darius*) to 1636 (*Love's Mistress*). Hazlitt, in his *Manual for the Collector*, makes frequent reference to the list. Its particular value lies in its early date of compilation.

1671 KIRKMAN'S CATALOGUE

6 [Kirkman, Francis.] *A True, perfect and exact Catalogue of all the Come-dies, Tragedies, Tragi-Comedies, Pastorals, Masques and Interludes, that were ever yet Printed and Published, till this present year 1671.* all which you may either buy or sell, at the Shop of Francis Kirkman, in Thames-street, over-against the Custom House, London [1671] 16 p

This catalogue, which is bibliographically independent, is found in, *Nicomede. A Tragi-Comedy, translated out of the French of Monsieur Corneille, by John Dancer. As it was acted at the Theatre Royal, in Dublin. Together with an Exact Catalogue of all the English Stage-Plays printed,* till this present year 1671 . . . Printed for Francis Kirkman, and are to be sold at his Shop in Thames-street over against the Custom-House. 1671. [4] 56 16 p

808 plays are listed. This is far from a perfect catalogue, but Kirkman's main intention was to list the books which he had for sale and to bring his former catalogue of 1661 up to date. Basically, the same system is used as in the former catalogue, except that Kirkman now inserts works by the following authors in first place: Shakespeare, Beaumont and Fletcher, Johnson, Shirley, Heywood, Middleton, Rowley, Massinger, Chapman, Brome, and D'Avenant.

1675 PHILLIPS' THEATRUM POETARUM

7 Phillips, Edward. *Theatrum Poetarum, Or A Compleat Collection of the Poets, Especially The most-Eminent, of all Ages. The Antients distinguish't from the Moderns in their several Alphabets. With some Observations and Reflections upon many of them, particularly those of our own Nation. To-gether With a Prefatory Discourse of the Poets and Poetry in Generall. . . .* London, Printed for Charles Smith, at the Angel near the Inner Temple-Gate in Fleet-Street, Anno Dom. M.DC.LXXV. [36] 192 261 [3] p

169 authors of plays are included. The only reason for including this particular work, which is devoted to the lives of ancient and modern writers of poetry, both English and foreign, is that many of his attributions were adopted by Winstanley in his *Lives of the Most Famous English Poets* (1687) and is the source for a number of statements by Langbaine. For the plays which are noted, Phillips used Kirkman's *Catalogue* of 1671. The work is arranged alphabetically according to the first name; when a group of writers have the same first name, the surnames are then arranged in alphabetical order. Thus, the work is difficult to use. It is also superficial and unreliable for dramatic material. Dates are not generally used and comments tend to be somewhat vacuous.

10

8 Baugh, Albert C. "A Seventeenth Century Play-List," *Modern Language Review* XIII (October 1918) 401–411

210 plays are listed. Professor Baugh reproduces the contents of this manuscript of eleven leaves, belonging to Anthony à Wood and located at the Bodleian Library. It is a catalogue of plays belonging to Mr. Horne, Fellow of Oriel College, and after his death passing to Mr. John Houghton of Brasenose, then to Mr. Hernes of St. Alds parish, and finally to R. Sheldon, of Weston. Between the dates of 1599 and 1643, the manuscript lists 210 plays by name. For each play the manuscript gives: 1) Title; 2) Author; 3) City of publication; 4) Date of the publication of the play. The value, of course, lies primarily in the date it was apparently gathered together.

[after 1677] ABRAHAM HILL'S LIST

9 Adams, J. Q. "Hill's List of Early Plays in Manuscript," *Library* 4th ser XX (June 1939) 71–99

51 plays listed. The list of early plays is found in one of Abraham Hill's ten note books, written on one leaf. A commentary is given for each of the fifty-one titles listed. In addition, on the verso of the same sheet, Hill listed twenty-six plays. In both lists authors are included for a number of the plays. In the first list authors' names are appended to thirteen of the plays. The second list gives twenty-six plays, all published in or before 1677 and all except eight of them pre-Restoration in date of composition. Adams discusses each of the plays, some of which are known only from this list. The manuscript is in the British Museum. The main reason for including the list is its fairly early date.

1680 LANGBAINE'S EXACT CATALOGUE

10 [Langbaine, Gerard.] *An Exact Catalogue of All the Comedies, Tragedies, Tragi-Comedies, Operas, Masks, Pastorals, and Interludes That were ever yet Printed and Published, till this present year 1680.* Oxon, Printed for L. Lichfield, Printer to the University, for Nicholas Cox, Anno Dom. 1680. 16 p

Basically this work is a reprint with additions of Kirkman's *Catalogue* of 1671. For years there has been some question of Langbaine's authorship. It seems, however, to belong to Langbaine for, although his name does not appear on the title page, he does claim the work as his own on p 395 and 409 of his *An Account Of The English Dramatick Poets* (1691). Since this claim was never challenged by any of Langbaine's contemporaries, there seems to be no reason to doubt his statement.

The catalogue has a list of titles in two alphabets with one ending in 1675 and the other, which gives a list of additions with authors' names added, running from 1675 to 1680. For a study of the work see the article by Hugh Macdonald, "Gerard Langbaine The Younger and Nicholas Cox." *Library* XXV (June – Sept 1944) 67–70; XXV (Dec – March 1944–45) 186.

1687 WINSTANLEY'S LIVES

11 Winstanley, William. *The Lives Of the most Famous English Poets, Or The Honour of Parnassus; In a Brief Essay Of above Two Hundred of them, from the Time of K. William the Conqueror, To the Reign of His Present Majesty King James II* . . . Written by William Winstanley, Author of the *English Worthies.* Licensed, June 16, 1686. Rob. Midgley. London, Printed by H. Clark, for Samuel Manship at the Sign of the Black Bull in Cornhil 1687. [24] 221 p

467 plays by 60 authors are noted in the work. This study of the poets is based primarily on Phillips' *Theatrum Poetarum* (1675) and copies some of the same errors. Although the work is not a list of dramas or dramatists, it is included here because it does list some

sixty men who were dramatists with the titles of their plays and because it forms a basis for later lists of plays.

The arrangement is chronological for the authors. For each author a brief life is given with a mention of the writer's poems or plays. The index lists the authors in the order in which they appear in the volume. Today the list is of little value for dramatists and their plays, although Winstanley is one of the first to mention that Thomas Heywood had a hand in some 200 plays.

There is a facsimile reproduction of this edition, with an introduction by William Riley Parker, published in 1963 at Gainesville, Florida, for Scholars' Facsimiles & Reprints.

1688 LANGBAINE'S MOMUS TRIUMPHANS

12 Langbaine, Gerard. *Momus Triumphans: Or, The Plagiaries Of The English Stage: Expos'd in a Catalogue Of All The Comedies, Tragi-Comedies, Masques, Tragedies, Opera's, Pastorals, Interludes, &c. Both Ancient and Modern, that were ever yet Printed in English. The Names of their Known and Supposed Authors. Their several Volumes and Editions: With an Account of the various Originals, as well English, French, and Italian, as Greek and Latine, from whence most of them have Stole their Plots.* By Gerard Langbaine, Esq. . . . London, Printed for Nicholas Cox, and are to be Sold by him in Oxford MDCLXXXVIII. xvi 32 [8] p

970 plays are listed and 129 authors. This, the first list published under Langbaine's name, has always caused some confusion. The edition was a surreptitious one, coming out in November 1687 (?), and Langbaine insisted that the title be changed to "A New Catalogue." A month later, in December, the new edition, together with the revised title, appeared. This particular edition, which sold some 500 copies, appeared with two different imprints, the second one reading: London, Printed for N. C. and are to be Sold by Sam. Holford at the Crown in Pall-Mall 1688. This particular imprint is located at Newberry library. In 1691 a new edition with many new entries appeared. Later the work was reprinted with more editions by Giles Jacobs and published in 1719.

Because the material in this work and in the *New Catalogue* are the same, an assessment of it will be made in the next entry.

1688 LANGBAINE'S NEW CATALOGUE

13 Langbaine, Gerard. *A New Catalogue of English Plays, Containing All the Comedies, Tragedies, Tragi-Comedies, Opera's, Masques, Pastorals, Interludes, Farces, &c. Both Ancient and Modern, that have ever yet been Printed, to this present year, 1688. To which, are added, The Volumes, and best Editions; with divers Remarks, of the Originals of most Plays; and the Plagiaries of several Authors.* By Gerard Langbaine, Gent . . . London, Printed for Nicholas Cox, and are to be Sold by him in Oxford MDCLXXXVIII. xvi 32 [8] p

970 plays are listed and 129 authors. Langbaine sets out to correct the numerous errors found in earlier catalogues which had inserted titles of plays supposedly in print but which, in reality, had never been printed. In addition he attempted: 1) to point out repetitions in these lists; 2) to point out errors of ascription, particularly in regard to anonymous plays; 3) to point out omissions. Thus, he does actually correct many of the errors in these earlier catalogues. Yet, in spite of his attempt to be accurate, numerous errors remain.

The volume is divided as follows: 1) Authors alphabetically arranged according to surnames, together with their plays; 2) Supposed authors; 3) Unknown authors. For each play Langbaine gives: 1) Author; 2) Title; 3) Type; 4) Format. In addition, for some plays he gives a brief note regarding the source. 165 of the 970 plays listed are anonymous. Of the 129 authors, 103 are known and 26 are supposed authors.

1691 Langbaine's English Dramatick Poets

14 Langbaine, Gerard. *An Account of the English Dramatick Poets. Or, Some Observations and Remarks On the Lives and Writings, of all those that have Publish'd either Comedies, Tragedies, Tragi-Comedies, Pastorals, Masques, Interludes, Farces, or Opera's in the English Tongue.* By Gerard Langbaine. Oxford, Printed by L. L. for George West, and Henry Clements, An. Dom. 1691. [16] 556 [36] p

970 plays are listed and 205 authors. Basically this work is an enlargement of his *New Catalogue*, with indexes of authors and of plays. What is interesting is that a count of plays as listed in the index to this volume gives the same total number of plays as are to be found in the *New Catalogue*. And yet 205 authors appear in this work and only 129 in the *New Catalogue*.

This, his most important work, is arranged alphabetically by author and the entries extend to 1691. The treatment of the various authors ranges from seven lines (Thomas Ingeland) to forty-seven pages (John Dryden). Each entry is devoted to a short account of the life of the writer followed by an account of each play. For each play Langbaine gives: 1) Title; 2) Type; 3) Theatre; 4) Date printed; 5) Format; 6) Source; 7) Comments on play, ranging from a line or two to more than a page. In regard to the sources for various plays Langbaine gives some brilliant "hits" and "misses." Because of the "misses," however, the work should be used with some caution. It is honest and is regarded by historians of the drama as the first fairly reliable catalogue. It becomes "the basis of all subsequent catalogues down to and including Hazlitt's *Manual*." Langbaine's sources are Phillips, Winstanley, Fuller, Lloyd, and Wood.

A second ed was published by Charles Gildon in 1698 with some of the copies dated 1699. A third ed appeared in 1751. For its effect on later compilers, see: Alun Watkins-Jones, "Langbaine's Account of the English Dramatick Poets (1691)" *Essays and Studies* xxi (1936) 75–85. In 1958 the *Account* was edited, with introduction and notes, by John Joseph McCall as a Ph.D. dissertation at Florida State University.

1699 Gildon's English Dramatick Poets

15 [Gildon, Charles.] *The Lives and Characters Of The English Dramatick Poets. Also An Exact Account of all the Plays that were ever yet Printed in the English Tongue; their Double Titles, the Places where Acted, the Dates when Printed, and the Persons to whom Dedicated; with Remarks and Observations on most of the said Plays. First begun by Mr. Langbaine, improv'd and continued down to this Time, by a Careful Hand.* London, Printed for Nich. Cox, and William Turner, and are to be sold at the White House without Temple-Bar 1699. [16] 182 [13] p

1,112 plays are listed and 259 authors. It first appeared in 1698 with no date on the title-page. The 1699 date is supposed to cover a reissue. In the preface, Charles Gildon, to whom it is usually ascribed, says that the work was not all by one hand and that in a few cases he himself has had access to plays not seen by Langbaine. Basically, it is a digest, abridgment, and continuation of Langbaine's 1691 edition. Although it does mention several authors and works not found in Langbaine, the improvements are negligible and its value lies in its continuation of the former work. The entries for printed plays are continued to 1698. For each play he gives: 1) Title; 2) Account of the plot; 3) Staging; 4) Merits and defects of the play; 5) Date; 6) Format; 7) Theatre; 8) Sources. It was printed once again in 1751.

1708 Downes' Roscius Anglicanus

16 [Downes, John.] *Roscius Anglicanus, Or, An Historical Review Of The Stage. After it had been Suppress'd by means of the late Unhappy Civil War, begun in 1641, 'till the Time of King Charles the IId's. Restoration, in May, 1660.*

Giving an Account of its Rise again; of the Times and Places the Governours of both the Companies first erected their Theatres. The Names of the Principal Actors and Actresses, who Performed in the Chiefest Plays in each House. With the Names of the most taking Plays, and Modern Poets, for the space of 46 Years, and during the Reign of Three Kings, and part of our present Sovereign Lady, Queen Anne, from 1660 to 1706. . . . London, Printed and Sold by H. Playford, at his House in Arundel-Street, near the Water-side 1708. [4] 52 p

241 plays are listed. It is basically a history of the stage during the years 1660 to 1706 and its chief value lies in that fact. Because it does list some 241 plays for this period, however, and because it is a basic reference source for theatre history of the period, it is included here. As there is no index, the number of plays was obtained by counting those listed on each page. Further, the 241 plays listed are not all plays written between 1660 and 1706 as a fair number are revivals of plays written before 1660.

In 1789 there was an edition with additions by Thomas Davies and edited by Francis Godolphin Waldron. Two other editions have been published since then: one by Joseph Knight in 1886 is a facsimile reprint and the other in 1928, edited by Montague Summers, attempts to give explanatory notes concerning each play mentioned. The annotated edition by Summers is superior to the Waldron edition, although Summers has a number of fanciful conjectures.

1713 MEARS' EXACT CATALOGUE

17 [Mears, W.] *A True and Exact Catalogue Of All the Plays That were ever yet Printed in the English Tongue; with the Authors Names against each Play (Alphabetically Digested) and continued down to October, 1713.* London, Printed for W. Mears at the Lamb without Temple-bar 1713. 48 p

1,325 plays are listed. The *Catalogue* is an alphabetical listing of plays by title followed by an indication of the type of play and, when known, the last name of the author. There are a few cross references to avoid duplication. Although it does give the largest number of titles of plays to date, it does not give dates, the various editions of a work, or theatre information relative to staging. Further, the *Catalogue* does copy some of the old errors relative to authorship. It should be used simply as a title listing.

Clark Sutherland Northup, in *A Register Of Bibliographies Of The English Language and Literature* (New York 1925), says that "In 1715, a new issue of the catalogue, apparently, was made by prefixing a single sheet, with the title: Continuation of the Following Catalogue of Plays to October, 1715. To Which is Prefix'd a Catalogue of Plays, Printed in 12-mo. with a Neat Elziver Letter. Sold by W. Mears at the Lamb without Temple-Bar. Of whom May be Had Above Five Hundred Several Sorts of Plays, in 4 to and 12 mo" (p 139).

1719 JACOB'S POETICAL REGISTER

18 [Jacob, Giles.] *The Poetical Register: Or, The Lives and Characters of the English Dramatick Poets. With An Account Of Their Writings.* London, Printed for E. Curll, in Fleetstreet MDCCXIX. [26] 433 [22] p

1,439 plays are listed and 294 authors. Some copies vary in initial and final pagination. It is arranged alphabetically by author with a brief account of each writer, together with a list of his plays. The foundation for this work is Langbaine's, with some dependence upon later catalogues. He attempts to correct some of the errors in Langbaine's volume. A number of the accounts of contemporaries, Jacob says, were contributed by the writers themselves. There is an index of authors as well as an index of plays. For each play he gives: 1) Title; 2) Type; 3) Theatre; 4) Date of performance; 5) Source when known; 6) Brief general remarks. In all, this is a very honest work and still of some value.

"The sheets of this edition were issued in 1723 with a new title page, by A. Bettesworth and, in 1724, by W. Mears. In these issues *The Poetical Register* is made a companion volume to *An Historical Account of the Lives and Writings of Our Most Considerable English Poets.*" In the 1723 issue, the "Register" is found in vol one; in the 1724 issue, the "Register" is found in vol two. Further, in the 1724 issue, the preliminary material is rearranged but is not changed as to content or number of plays.

1719 MEARS' COMPLEAT CATALOGUE

19 [Mears, W.] *A Compleat Catalogue Of all the Plays That were ever yet Printed in the English Language. Containing the Dates, and the Number of Plays Written by every particular Author: An Account of what Plays were Acted with Applause, and of those which were never Acted; and also of the Authors now living. In two separate Alphabets.* London, Printed for W. Mears at the Lamb without Temple-Bar 1719. Price 1s sticht. Where may be had great Variety of Plays. 95 p

1,486 plays are listed and 280 authors. The arrangement is much better than in the 1713 edition and is now divided into two sections as follows: 1) Author entries in alphabetical order, with the plays by the individual author in chronological order, and the type of play indicated each time; 2) Plays entered in alphabetical order, which are printed in English, and "Continu'd down to June, 1718," with the type of play and author noted. Some of the old errors in regard to attribution, however, still persist. It was reissued in 1726 with a continuation to that year.

1726 MEARS' COMPLEAT CATALOGUE

20 [Mears, W.] *A Compleat Catalogue of All the Plays That were ever yet Printed In the English Language. Containing The Dates and Number of Plays Written by every particular Author: An Account of what Plays were Acted with Applause, and of those which were never Acted; and also the Authors now living. In Two separate Alphabets. Continued to this present year, 1726.* The Second Edition. London, Printed for W. Mears, at the Lamb without Temple-Bar M.DCCXXVI. Price One Shilling stich'd. 104 p

1,654 plays are listed. It is a reprinting to p 95 of the 1719 edition. The last leaf of the 1719 edition (p 95–96) was removed, a new leaf was substituted, and p 97–104 containing the appendix, which continued the list of plays from 1718 to 1726, were added. 168 new titles are listed in the appendix which gives the title of the play, the type, and the author. Mears' work was used by some later compilers who continued to perpetuate some of his errors of attribution.

1732 FEALES' CATALOGUE

21 [Feales, W.] *A True and Exact Catalogue Of all the Plays And other Dramatic Pieces, That were ever yet Printed in the English Tongue, In Alphabetical Order: Continu'd down to April 1732.* London, Printed for W. Feales, at Rowe's Head over against-Clement's-inn Gate 1732. 35 p

The catalogue, which is bibliographically independent, is bound with Ben Jonson's *The Three celebrated Plays Of that Excellent Poet Ben Johnson. Viz. The Fox, a Comedy. The Alchymist, a Comedy. The Silent Woman, a Comedy. To which is added, A compleat Catalogue of all the Plays that were ever printed in the English Language, to the Year 1732.* London, Printed for W. Feales at Rowe's Head, over-against Clement's-Inn Gate [1732]. [2] 96 96 100 35 p

1,737 plays are listed. The catalogue, which gives the largest number of play titles to date, is merely an alphabetical list of titles which, in its general arrangement, imitates Mears' *Catalogue* of 1713. It gives neither the names of authors, dates, format, or theatrical history, but merely indicates the type of play. Plays with the same titles are not distinguished from one another in any way. Starred plays are "Acting Plays." It may be a bookseller's list, although I have no proof for this conjecture.

22   Whincop, Thomas. *Scanderbeg: Or, Love and Liberty. Written by the late Thomas Whincop, Esq. To which are added A List of all the Dramatic Authors, with some Account of their Lives; and of all the Dramatic Pieces ever published in the English Language, to the year 1747.* London, Printed for W. Reeve at Shakespear's Head, Serpent's-Inn-Gate, in Fleet-street MDCCXLVII. xix [3] 320 [30] p

The title of the list, which is attributed to John Mottley, is: "A Compleat List Of all the English Dramatic Poets, And of All the Plays ever printed in the English Language, To The Present year M,DCC,XLVII."

1,766 plays are listed and 357 authors. As Whincop died in 1730, the list was "nominally edited by his widow Martha." The entire work, however, appears to have been revised by John Mottley. The list is based in large part upon Jacob's *Poetical Register*, with some influence from Charles Gildon's *The Lives and Characters Of The English Dramatick Poets*.

The "List" is arranged in two divisions as follows: 1) Authors before the Restoration, with a short biographical account of each writer and his plays arranged in chronological order; 2) Authors since the Restoration, with a short biographical account of each writer and his plays arranged in chronological order. Anonymous pieces are placed at the conclusion of each section. For each play he gives: 1) Title; 2) Type, 3) Theatre; 4) Date of published edition; 5) Facts relative to source or circumstance of composition, when available. Two indexes are inserted, one of authors before and since the Restoration and another of all plays which are listed. Because of the number of errors and inaccuracies the work must be used with caution.

1750   Chetwood's British Theatre

23   [Chetwood, William Rufus.] *The British Theatre. Containing The Lives of the English Dramatic Poets; With An Account of all their Plays. Together With The Lives of most of the Principal Actors, as well as Poets. To which is prefixed, A short View of the Rise and Progress of the English Stage.* Dublin, Printed for Peter Wilson, in Dame-street   M.DCC,L. [2] 16 [6] 200 [28] p

1,927 plays are listed in the index and 397 authors. The work extends from 1538 to 1750 and is arranged by chronological periods according to the reigning monarch. Within each period the authors are arranged in chronological order, according to year of birth. After a few introductory remarks for each writer, there follows a list of the plays, with an indication of the date of performance or of publication. Indexes of authors and of plays are included. The work must be referred to with great caution as the writer frequently uses conjecture instead of fact, not only for dates of production and printed editions but also for attribution of anonymous plays. Stephen Jones, in the 1812 edition of the *Biographia Dramatica*, accuses Chetwood of deliberately forging and creating dates and titles (I LXXIII). The Folger Shakespeare Library copy frequently supplies the correct date in ink as well as many of the omissions.

Another issue appeared in 1752, with the London imprint, printed for R. Baldwin, Jr. In 1756 the work was reprinted at Dublin for Peter Wilson and included in *A Companion To The Theatre: Or, A View of our most celebrated Dramatic Pieces. In which the Plan, Characters, and Incidents of each are particularly explained. Interspersed with Remarks Historical, Critical and Moral. To which is added, [not in any other edition], A brief Account of the Lives and Writings of the English*, etc.

[1750–1760?]   Warburton's List of Plays

24   Greg, W. W. "The Bakings of Betsy," *The Library* 3rd Ser II (1911) 225–259

57 plays are listed. Greg gives a copy of John Warburton's list of manuscript plays, with a study of the whole problem of the plays and their existence. The value of the list lies particularly in the titles of the plays which were supposedly in manuscript. In fact, these

titles have intrigued scholars for years. The list of plays is divided into two sections, with the first containing forty-one titles, of which one is scratched out. The second list follows Warburton's explanation that these manuscript plays were destroyed by his servant in a fire. There follows a list of seventeen plays in manuscript. Greg examines all the evidence objectively.

1753   CIBBER'S LIVES OF THE POETS

25   Cibber, [Theophilus.] *The Lives of The Poets of Great Britain and Ireland, To the Time of Dean Swift. Compiled from ample Materials scattered in a Variety of Books, and especially from the MS. Notes of the late ingenious Mr. Coxeter and others, collected for this Design.* By Mr. Cibber. In Four Volumes. London, Printed for R. Griffiths, at the Dunciad in St. Paul's Churchyard 1753. 5 vols

811 plays are listed and 212 authors of plays. It is included in this survey because 212 of the authors did write plays. The lives of the authors are arranged in chronological order, beginning with Geoffrey Chaucer. For each playwright, after a brief life history, Cibber lists the individual plays of the writer, together with brief comments on the play. As sources for the work he uses Phillips, Winstanley, Chetwood, Langbaine, and the manuscript notes of Chetwood. It is of some value for the history of an individual play's reception. A number of old errors, however, are perpetuated because he frequently accepts the attributions found in his sources, without attempting to discover the identity of the authors by the use of factual evidence.

1756   CIBBER'S APOLOGY

26   Cibber, Colley. *An Apology for the Life of Colley Cibber, Comedian. Written by Himself . . . The Fourth Edition. . . . With an Account of the Rise and Progress of the English Stage: a Dialogue on Old Plays, and Old Players; and a List of Dramatic Authors and Their Works.* London, Printed for R. and J. Dodsley 1756. 2 vols

1,659 plays are listed and 414 authors. See Vol 2 (p 169–303) which contains the "List of Dramatic Authors and Their Works." Basically it is the same work printed from the same setting of type but with a different title page, pagination, and signatures, as the *Theatrical Records* of 1756. The whole is based upon Chetwood's *The British Theatre*, although the latter work has more play titles. Extending from 1538 to 1756, it is arranged in roughly chronological order. There are indexes of authors and of plays. Authorship of the "List of Dramatic Authors" has been variously attributed to William Chetwood himself and to Robert Dodsley, but there is no proof. Most of the errors found in Chetwood's *The British Theatre* remain uncorrected. As a result its value is slight.

1756   THE THEATRICAL RECORDS

27   *Theatrical Records: Or, An Account of English Dramatic Authors, and Their Works.* London, Printed for R. and J. Dodsley, at Tully's Head in Pall-mall 1756. 135 [1] 32 p

1,830 plays are listed and 417 authors. This work, as was the preceding, is divided into chronological periods with authors listed in more or less chronological order within the period and plays listed in chronological order under the name of the author. Each section also contains a division for anonymous authors. Indexes of authors and of plays make the volume easier to use than would be otherwise possible with a chronological arrangement. For each play the compiler gives: 1) Title; 2) Type; 3) Date of publication. Chetwood's influence is to be seen throughout. For this reason and because the dates are frequently incorrect, as are the spellings for names of various plays, it must be used with great caution. Stephen Jones, in the 1812 edition of the *Biographia Dramatica*, says it is "unworthy of the smallest regard" (ɪ LXXIII).

28   Victor, [Benjamin.]   *The History Of The Theatres Of London and Dublin, From the Year 1730 to the present Time, To which is added, An Annual Register Of all the Plays, &c. performed at the Theatres-Royal in London, from the Year 1721.*   With Occasional Notes and Anecdotes By Mr. Victor, Late one of the Managers of the Theatre-Royal in Dublin. London, Printed for T. Davies, in Russel-street, Covent-Garden; R. Griffiths, T. Becket, and P. A. De Hondt, in the Strand; G. Woodfall, at Charing-Cross; J. Coote, in Pater-noster-row; and G. Kearsly in Ludgate-street   MDCCLXI. 2 vols

255 plays are listed. The "Annual Register," which begins in 1713 and ends in 1759, lists 191 plays. An annual register for Lincoln's-Inn-Fields and Covent-Garden Theatres does not have the same time span as the one for the Theatres-Royal but extends only from 1713 to 1731 and lists 64 plays. A third volume, although not called such, was published in 1771 (see under that date). These histories were continued to 1817 by Walley Chamberlain Oulton. Victor's work has been variously praised and condemned.

1764   BAKER'S COMPANION TO THE PLAY-HOUSE

29   [Baker, David Erskine.]   *The Companion To The Play-House: Or, An Historical Account of all the Dramatic Writers (and their Works) that have appeared in Great Britain and Ireland, From The Commencement of our Theatrical Exhibitions, down to the Present Year 1764. Composed in the Form of a Dictionary, For the more readily turning to any particular Author, or Performance.*   In Two Volumes. Vol I Contains, A Critical and Historical Account of every Tragedy, Comedy, Farce, &c., in the English Language. The respective Merits of each Piece, and of the Actors who performed the principal Characters, are particularly examined and pointed out. Vol II Contains, The Lives and Productions of every Dramatic Writer for the English Or Irish Theatres, including not only all those Memoirs that had been formerly written, but also a great Number of new Lives and curious Anecdotes never before communicated to the Public. Also the Lives of our most celebrated Actors, who were likewise Authors of any Theatrical Composition from Shakespeare and Johnson, down to the present Time. London, Printed for T. Becket and P. A. Dehondt, in the Strand; C. Henderson, at the Royal Exchange; and T. Davies, in Russel-Street, Covent-Garden 1764. 2 vols

2,233 plays are listed and 453 authors. The work is generally ascribed to David Erskine Baker. Vol I lists the plays. For each play the author gives: 1) Title; 2) Type; 3) Author; 4) Format; 5) Date of publication or printing; 6) Theatre; 7) Judgment of a play's worth for a number of works, as well as source when known. Vol II gives the lives of the 453 authors in alphabetical order, together with a list of the plays by each writer. In this volume the author adopts Langbaine's alphabetical arrangement in the account of the authors. Further, the author uses Langbaine and Whincop as authorities as well as Coxeter's manuscript notes. There is no doubt about the honesty of the work and the fine view it gives of contemporary plays, but some of the old errors still persist. Isaac Reed corrects a number of these errors in his edition of 1782.

1771   VICTOR'S HISTORY OF THE THEATRES

30   Victor, [Benjamin.]   *The History Of The Theatres Of London, From the Year 1760 to the present Time. Being A Continuation of the Annual Register of all the new Tragedies, Comedies, Farces, Pantomimes, &c. that have been per-*

formed within that Period. With Occasional Notes and Anecdotes. By Mr. Victor, Author of the two former Volumes. London, Printed for T. Becket, in the Strand MDCCLXXI. [3] iv–xi [1] 232 p

122 plays are listed. The *Annual Register* is for the period from September 1760 to February 23 1771 at the Theatre Royal, Drury Lane, Covent-Garden Theatre, and the Hay-Market, which is noted in the appendix. For each play Victor gives: 1) Theatre; 2) Date; 3) Title; 4) Author; 5) Remarks on the author and/or the play; 6) Reaction of the audience and, at times, the length of the run. It is a valuable list for the period, although such later works as Reed's edition of the *Biographia Dramatica* and Egerton's *Theatrical Remembrancer* supplant it.

1779 PLAYHOUSE POCKET-COMPANION

31 *The Playhouse Pocket-Companion, Or Theatrical Vade-Mecum: Containing, I. A Catalogue of all the Dramatic Authors who have written for the English Stage, with a List of their Works, shewing the Dates of Representation or Publication. II. A Catalogue of Anonymous Pieces. III. An Index of Plays and Authors. In a Method entirely new, Whereby the Author of any Dramatic Performance, and the Time of its Appearance, may be readily discovered on Inspection. To which is prefixed, a Critical History of the English Stage from its Origin to the present Time; with an Enquiry into the Causes of the Decline of Dramatic Poetry in England.* London, Printed and sold by Messers. Richardson and Urquhart, under the Royal Exchange, Cornhill; J. Wenman, No. 144, Fleet Street; and J. Southern, in St. James's Street 1779. [4] [13]–179 p

2,224 plays and 507 authors. 400 of the plays are anonymous. The catalogue proper is arranged alphabetically by author, with the author's individual plays listed under his name in chronological order. For each play the compiler gives: 1) Title; 2) Type; 3) Date of production or printing; 4) Judgment as to a play's worth at various times. As it is based upon Chetwood's *British Theatre* and retains a number of the errors found in that work, it should be used with caution. In fact, Stephen Jones, in the 1812 edition of the *Biographia Dramatica*, says that it is "Not to be trusted" (I LXXIII).

[1779] CAPELL'S NOTITIA DRAMATICA

32 [Capell, Edward.] *Notitia Dramatica; or, Tables of Ancient Plays, (from their Beginning, to the Restoration of Charles the second) so many as have been printed, with their several Editions: faithfully compiled, and digested in quite new Method,* By E. C. With a Preface. In: *Notes and Various Readings to Shakespeare. . . .* London, Printed by Henry Hughs, for the Author [1779]. 3 vols

764 plays are listed and 215 authors. The work, which is an original one and of value, depends upon Langbaine and upon "modern sale-catalogues." The author uses an asterisk to indicate what information he has taken from these works. The "Notitia" is in Vol III and has a four-fold division as follows: 1) An alphabetical list of plays; 2) Alphabetical list of collected editions; 3) Alphabetical list of authors, with their plays, and a table of joint authorship; 4) Chronological list of authors and anonymous plays. For each play the author gives: 1) Title; 2) Author; 3) Date; 4) Printer and publisher of each edition known to the compiler; 5) Format. What makes this work of particular value are the various editions given for an individual play.

1782 REED'S BIOGRAPHIA DRAMATICA

33 [Reed, Isaac.] *Biographia Dramatica, Or, A Companion To The Playhouse: Containing Historical and Critical Memoirs, and Original Anecdotes, of Brit-*

*ish and Irish Dramatic Writers, from the Commencement of the most cele-
brated Actors. Also An Alphabetical Account of their Works, the Dates when
printed, and occasional Observations on their Merits. Together With An Introductory View of the Rise and Progress of the British Stage.* By David Erskine
Baker, Esq. A New Edition: Carefully Corrected; greatly enlarged; and continued from 1764 to 1782. London, Printed for Messrs. Rivingtons, St. Paul's
Church-Yard; T. Payne and Son, Mews-Gate; L. Davis, Holborn; T. Longman, and G. Robinson, Pater Noster-Row; J. Dodsley, Pall-Mall; J. Nichols,
Red-Lion-Passage, Fleet-Street; J. Debret, Piccadilly; and T. Evans, in the
Strand 1782. 2 vols

3,507 plays are listed and 756 authors. This is a revised edition by Isaac Reed of Baker's
Companion to the Playhouse (1764). In all there are 3,312 English plays, 37 Latin plays
by Englishmen, 40 oratorios, and 118 additional plays in the appendix to Vol II. Vol I
contains a study of the dramatic writers and a list of their plays arranged in alphabetical
order by author. Vol II is an alphabetical listing of all the dramatic pieces. Each entry
is numbered, but the numbering begins anew with each letter of the alphabet. Cross
references are used. For each play Reed gives: 1) Title; 2) Type; 3) Author; 4) Format;
5) Date of publication; 6) Remarks on the play. The work is carefully done and many
of the errors in Baker's edition have been corrected. This edition is superseded, however,
by Stephen Jones' edition of 1812, which also corrects a number of errors which are in
Reed's work.

34 No entry

1788 EGERTON'S THEATRICAL REMEMBRANCER

35 Egerton, Thomas. *Egerton's Theatrical Remembrancer, Containing A Com-
plete List Of All The Dramatic Performances In The English Language; Their
Several Editions, Dates, And Sizes, And The Theatre Where They Were
Originally Performed: Together With An Account Of Those Which Have
Been Acted And Are Unpublished, And A Catalogue Of Such Latin Plays As
Have Been Written By English Authors. From The Earliest Production Of
The English Drama To The End Of The Year MDCCLXXXVIII. To Which
Are Added Notitia Dramatica, Being A Chronological Account Of Events Rela-
tive To The English Stage.* London, Printed for T. and J. Egerton, At The
Military Library, Whitehall MDCCLXXXVIII. vi [2] 354 p

3,728 plays are listed and 865 authors. A painstaking work, arranged chronologically by
author, beginning with John Rastell about 1510 and concluding with Harriet Lee's work
The New Peerage, or Our Eyes may deceive us in 1787. It is based upon the 1782 edition
of the *Biographia Dramatica* and upon Mears' *Catalogue.* In addition, F. W. Foster, in his
article, "Title List of Catalogues of English Plays" *Notes and Queries* 5th Ser XII (1879)
262, says that the work was compiled partly from J. Henderson's manuscripts and from
works in the libraries of J. Henderson, R. Wright, and T. Pearson. For each play Egerton
gives: 1) Title; 2) Type; 3) Acting Company or theatre; 4) Format; 5) Date of publication. If there is more than one edition he gives the dates of each. Sometimes the purpose
of the play is indicated; at times the Stationers' Register date is noted. Indexes of authors
and of plays allow the reader to locate a play without difficulty. In spite of the fact that
there are some errors in dating and attribution, as well as titles which are repeated, this
work is still useful. The Folger Shakespeare Library copy has notes by Edmund Malone.

1792 A NEW THEATRICAL DICTIONARY

36 *A New Theatrical Dictionary. Containing An Account Of All The Dramatic
Pieces That Have Appeared From The Commencement Of Theatrical Exhibitions To The Present Time. Together With Their Dates When Written Or*

Printed, where Acted, and Occasional Remarks on their Merits and Success. To Which Is Added An Alphabetical Catalogue Of Dramatic Writers, With The Titles of all the Pieces they have Written, annexed to each Name. And Also A Short Sketch of the Rise and Progress of the English Stage. London, Printed for S. Bladon, No. 13, Paternoster-Row 1792. [8] 400 p

2,983 plays are listed and 654 authors. It is basically an abridgement of Isaac Reed's *Biographia Dramatica* of 1782, with some of the errors of that work still remaining in regard to attribution and dating. For each play the compiler gives: 1) Title; 2) Author; 3) Theatre; 4) Format 5) Date of publication; 6) Brief critical remarks, often including source or indications of adaptation or translation. There are very few cross references. Its value today is questionable, for it does not contain as many plays as Egerton's *Theatrical Remembrancer* and later compilations have corrected many of its errors.

1796 OULTON'S HISTORY OF THE THEATRES

37 [Oulton, W. C.] *The History Of The Theatres of London: Containing An Annual Register Of All The New And Revised Tragedies, Comedies, Operas, Farces, Pantomimes, &c. That Have Been Performed At The Theatres Royal, in London, From the Year 1771 to 1795. With Occasional Notes and Anecdotes.* London, Printed for and sold by Martin and Bain, Fleet-street; Sold also by T. Egerton, Whitehall; W. Miller, Bond-Street; J. Bell, Oxford-street; and T. Boosey, Bond-street, near the Royal Exchange MDCCXCVI. 2 vols

630 plays are listed. It is a continuation of Benjamin Victor's *History of the Theatres of London* and begins on June 26 1771. The arrangement is chronological by month and day for each theatre. Not only does it note each play performed, including revivals, it also gives the audience reaction. Although the value for this particular survey of dramatic bibliographies may be questionable, as the titles of the plays are to be found in other works, it is necessary for a study of the theatre of the period. It extends to Sep 2 1795.

[1801] BARKER'S CONTINUATION OF EGERTON

38 Oulton, Walley Chamberlain. *Barker's Continuation of Egerton's Theatrical Remembrancer, Baker's Biographia Dramatica, &c. Containing, A complete List of all the Dramatic Performances their several Editions, Dates and Sizes, together with those which are unpublished, and the Theatres where they were originally performed; From MDCCLXXXVII to MDCCCI. Including several Omissions, Additions and Corrections, Also a Continuation of the Notitia Dramatica, With considerable Improvements. To Which Is Added A Complete List of Plays, The Earliest Date, Size, and Author's Name, (Where known.) From The Commencement To 1801.* The Whole arranged, &c. by Walley Chamberlain Oulton. London, Printed and Published by Barker & Son, Dramatic Repository, Great Russell Street, Covent Garden [1801?]. [4] 336 p

4,819 plays are listed. The most complete catalogue of plays to date, it is arranged in alphabetical order by title of the play. Such an arrangement, of course, makes an attempt to determine the number of authors impractical. P 1–102 are devoted to various additions from 1787 to 1800. Following this section is the "Complete List of all the plays &c. in the English Language, from the Earliest period to the present Time." For each play the compiler gives: 1) Title; 2) Type; 3) Format; 4) Date of first edition; 5) Author. When a number of plays have the same title they are listed in chronological order; frequently only the surname of the author will appear. Numerous cross references help in its use. The compiler does follow a number of the errors of his predecessors in regard to titles, dates, and attribution, although he has also corrected some of their mistakes. Basically, it is a good catalogue.

1802 THE THESPIAN DICTIONARY

39 *The Thespian Dictionary; Or, Dramatic Biography Of The Eighteenth Century; Containing Sketches of The Lives, Productions, &c. Of All The Principal Managers, Dramatists, Composers, Commentators, Actors, And Actresses, Of The United Kingdom: Interspersed with Several Original Anecdotes; And Forming A Concise History of the English Stage.* London, Printed by J. Cundee, Ivy-Lane, for T. Hurst, Paternoster-Row; W. Porter, and J. Archer, Dublin; and may be had of C. Chappell, Pall-Mall; and all the Booksellers 1802 [275] p

1,091 plays are listed and 214 authors. The dictionary is arranged in alphabetical order by author. Following each biography there is a list of the writer's dramatic works, the theatre where they were performed, and the date of performance. An uneven *Dictionary,* wherein the author omits minor writers, yet a basic reference work for the eighteenth century theatre. A second edition was published in 1805.

[1803] BARKER'S COMPLETE LIST

40 [Oulton, Walley Chamberlain.] *Barker's Complete List Of Plays, Exhibiting At One View, The Title, Size, Date, And Author, From The Commencement Of Theatrical Performances, To 1803. To Which Is Added A Continuation To the Theatrical Remembrancer, Designed To Shew Collectively Each Author's Work.* London, printed and published by [J.] Barker & Son, dramatic repository, [19] Great Russell Street, Covent Garden [1803]. [4] 350 p

This is a reissue of the 1801 edition with a new title-leaf and the added section, "Appendix To Barker's List of Plays, From The Commencement to 1803," p 337–350. 278 plays are added in this list. P 1–127 are entitled "Omissions, Additions, Correction, and Continuation to the Theatrical Remembrancer &." In this secion 1,021 plays are listed and 247 authors. For each play in this section the compiler gives: 1) Author; 2) Title; 3) Type; 4) Theatre; 5) Date of acting; 6) Format; 7) Date of publication. The other section has 4,576 plays and is entitled "A Complete List (Alphabetically arranged.) Of all the Plays,&c. in the English Language, from the earliest Period to the present Time; with the first Editions and Author's Names." The most complete work to date and basically good. Some libraries date their copies "[1804]."

1805 THE THESPIAN DICTIONARY

41 *The Thespian Dictionary; or, Dramatic Biography of the Present Age; containing Sketches of the Lives, Lists of the Productions, Various Merits, &c. &c. Of All the Principal Dramatists, Composers, Commentators, Managers, Actors, And Actresses, Of The United Kingdom: Interspersed with Numerous Original Anecdotes, Forming a Complete Modern History of The English Stage.* Second Edition, With Considerable Improvements And Additions. Illustrated by Twenty-Two Elegant Engravings. [London] Albion Press Printed: Published by James Cundee, Ivy-Lane, Paternoster-Row; Sold by C. Chapple, Pall-Mall 1805. [402] p

1,138 plays are listed and 223 authors. This second edition extends to the time of publication. Basically the arrangement for the volume is the same as in the 1802 edition. For each play the compiler generally gives: 1) Title; 2) Type; 3) Date; 4) Theatre; 5) Remarks on the success of the play. In spite of obvious weaknesses, it is still a reference work which must be consulted when working on the lives of actors and actresses, managers, and even authors of the period.

1808 Gilliland's Dramatic Mirror

42 Gilliland, Thomas. *The Dramatic Mirror: Containing the History of the Stage, From The Earliest Period To The Present Time; Including A Biographical and Critical Account Of All The Dramatic Writers, from 1660; And Also of The Most Distinguished Performers, From The Days of Shakespeare to 1807: And A History of The Country Theatres, In England, Ireland, And Scotland.* Embellished With Seventeen Elegant Engravings. London, Printed for C. Chapple, Pall Mall 1808. 2 vols paged continuously. xii 1048 p

520 authors. The work extends from 1660 to 1807. See vol I, "A Biographical and Critical Account of English Dramatic Writers, from the Restoration of Charles II. 1660, to the Year 1806," 250–630, where the authors are arranged in alphabetical order, with a list of plays written by each. If known, the date of the writing or acting of the play is given, but there is no information on publication. As a bibliography of plays its value is questionable and cannot be compared with the following compilation.

1812 Jones' Biographia Dramatica

43 Jones, Stephen. *Biographia Dramatica; Or, A Companion To The Playhouse: Containing Historical and Critical Memoirs, and original Anecdotes, Of British And Irish Dramatic Writers, From The Commencement Of Our Theatrical Exhibitions; Among Whom Are Some Of The Most Celebrated Actors: Also An Alphabetical Account, And Chronological Lists, Of Their Works, The Dates When Printed, And Observations On Their Merits: Together With An Introductory View Of The Rise And Progress Of The British Stage. Originally Compiled, To The Year 1764, By David Erskine Baker. Continued Thence to 1782, By Isaac Reed, F.A.S. And brought down to the End of November 1811, with very considerable Additions and Improvements throughout,* by Stephen Jones. London, Printed For T. Longman, Hurst, Rees, Orme, And Brown, T. Payne, G. and W. Nicol, Nichols And Son, Scotcherd and Letterman, J. Barker, W. Miller, R. H. Evans, J. Harding, J. Faulder, And Gale And Curtis 1812. 3 vols

6,203 plays are listed. Vol I, which is an alphabetical listing of authors, contains the lives of 557 authors. Vols II and III are devoted to an alphabetical listing of the plays. In the main the work is a reprint of Reed, although Jones has brought Reed's work up to date, and has corrected a number of errors which remained in the earlier work. For each play he gives: 1) Title; 2) Author; 3) Source; 4) Theatre; 5) Date of performance; 6) Format; 7) Date of first edition and of each following edition. Even though some errors still remain concerning attribution and dates of first editions, this is a standard work and highly useful.

1814 Barker's Drama Recorded

44 Barker, J. *The Drama Recorded; Or Barker's List of Plays, Alphabetically Arranged, Exhibiting At One View, The Title, Size, Date, and Author, With Their Various Alterations, From the Earliest Period, To 1814; To Which Are Added, Notitia Dramatica, Or, A Chronological Account of Events Relative To The English Stage.* London, Printed And Published By J. Barker, (Dramatic Repository,) Great Russell-Street, Covent-Garden 1814 [4] 212 p

6,740 plays are listed. Although the compiler has continued to follow a number of errors found in the earlier catalogues, he has corrected a number of inaccuracies concerned with attribution and date. Further, he gives the largest number of plays of any catalogue of English works prior to *The "Stage" Cyclopaedia* of 1909. The arrangement is alphabetical according to the title of the play. It is an expansion of the 1801 edition, *Barker's Continuation of Egerton's Theatrical Remembrancer.* For each play the compiler gives: 1) Title;

2) Type; 3) Format; 4) Date of Production or writing; 5) Author. Cross references are used. It is still of some value today although, for the period from 1660 to 1814, it is superseded by Allardyce Nicoll's work.

[1814] HASLEWOOD'S THE PROMPTER

45 [Haslewood, Joseph.] *The Prompter.* [London? Lee Priory Press? 1814?]. 308 p

5,107 plays are listed and 1,207 authors. A privately printed work which seems to exist in only one copy, located at the Folger Shakespeare Library, it follows the older division by century, beginning with 1500 A.D. and ending in 1813. Within each division the plays are listed in roughly chronological order of publication. A handwritten index of authors is bound in at the end. For each play the compiler attempts to give: 1) Title; 2) Date of staging; 3) Theatre; 4) Type; 5) Publisher; 6) Date of publication; 7) Source; 8) Any additional information available. An honest work, in which the compiler has attempted to be as accurate as possible. For a number of entries, however, he has had to depend upon earlier catalogues and, hence, a number of errors are repeated once again. For a discussion of the work see the present writer's article, "Problems in 'The Prompter,' a Guide to Plays" *Papers of the Bibliographical Society of America* LV (1961) 36–40.

1817 OULTON'S HISTORY OF THE THEATRES

46 Oulton, Walley Chamberlain. *A History of the Theatres of London, Containing An Annual Register Of New Pieces, Revivals, Pantomimes, &c. With Occasional Notes and Anecdotes. Being A Continuation Of Victor's & Oulton's Histories, From The Year 1795 to 1817 Inclusive.* By W. C. Oulton. London, Printed For C. Chapple, Pall-Mall; And W. Simpkin and R. Marshall, Stationers Court 1818. 3 vols

708 plays are listed. It is included in this survey because of its annual register of plays, which contains a daily calendar of plays, with some omissions, for the Theatres Royal. Vol I gives the register of the Theatre Royal, Drury Lane, from October 20 1795 to June 11 1817 and a total of 271 plays. Vol II gives the register of the Theatre Royal, Covent-Garden, from November 7 1795 to May 20 1817 and a total of 293 plays. Vol III gives the register of the Theatre Royal, Haymarket, and a treatment of English Opera, with a total of 144 plays. For each play Oulton gives: 1) Title; 2) Number of acts; 3) Author; 4) General remarks on the play or its reception. The work is still of some value for this period, particularly in regard to the reception the plays received.

1832 GENEST'S ACCOUNT OF THE ENGLISH STAGE

47 [Genest, John.] *Some Account of the English Stage, from the Restoration in 1660 to 1830.* Bath, Printed by H. E. Carrington 1832. 10 vols

3,571 plays are listed by title in the index. It is a chronological study of the daily performances at the Theatres Royal, Lincoln's Inn Fields, Dorset Garden, Haymarket, Goodman's Fields, Drury Lane Company, and Covent Garden Company. There is no basic format for his consideration of any individual play, but Genest does attempt to give, whenever possible, in addition to the name of the theatre and the date of performance, such facts or details about the play as contemporary judgment, source, name of the actors, or an outline of the plot. He does not hesitate to pass judgment on the play's worth. It is, by far, the most complete treatment of the period and is an absolutely necessary reference work for anyone working in it. For the period 1660 to 1800, in regard to accuracy of details concerning daily performances as well as actors, the work is being gradually superseded by the volumes of *The London Stage* which cover 1660–1800. It also exists in microprint.

1860 HALLIWELL'S DICTIONARY

48 Halliwell, James O. *A Dictionary of Old English Plays, Existing Either In Print Or In Manuscript, From the Earliest Times to The Close of The Seven-*

teenth Century; Including Also Notices Of Latin Plays Written By English Authors During the Same Period. London, John Russell Smith 1860. [8] 296 p

2,450 plays are listed and 537 authors. Arranged alphabetically by title of play, it is based primarily on the 1812 edition of the *Biographia Dramatica* and attempts to correct errors in that work. It is true that Halliwell has succeeded in correcting a number of errors as well as making some additions and alterations, but the compilation is a more or less perfunctory one which omits some plays. The list is restricted mainly to plays existing either in print or in manuscript, whether in English, written before 1700, or in Latin, if composed by English authors. For each play he attempts to give: 1) Title; 2) Type; 3) Author; 4) Theatre; 5) Format; 6) Date of first edition; 7) Notes on such matters as source, history of the play on the stage, or manuscript location when known.

1867 HAZLITT'S HAND-BOOK

49 Hazlitt, W. Carew. *Hand-Book To The Popular, Poetical, And Dramatic Literature of Great Britain, From the Invention of Printing to the Restoration.* London, John Russell Smith, Soho Square 1867. xii 701 [3] p

The arrangement of the *Hand-Book* is alphabetical according to the surname of the author, although anonymous works are also entered within the alphabetical listing. As it is devoted to writers and works which extend beyond the dramatic, there is no reason to attempt to determine the number of plays and authors of plays. Yet, since it does contain a good number of dramatic writers it must be included in this survey. For each author, Hazlitt gives the individual plays arranged in chronological order of publication with each play numbered. For each play he gives: 1) Full title; 2) Imprint; 3) Format; 4) Later editions; 5) Comments relative to attribution, editions, or staging. Copies of plays located at the British Museum and the Bodleian are noted. 94 anonymous works are listed under "Plays (Anonymous)." Because Hazlitt actually handled a good number of the plays and appended notes to these entries, it still has a certain value as well as interest.

1868 INGLIS' DRAMATIC WRITERS OF SCOTLAND

50 Inglis, Ralston. *The Dramatic Writers of Scotland.* Glasgow, G. D. Mackellar, 18 Renfield St. 1868. [2] 155 [1] p

785 plays by 375 authors are listed. It is arranged alphabetically by author with a brief life of each author, together with a list of his works. In addition to the 785 plays by known authors, there are 95 anonymous plays, making a total of 880 to 1868 inclusive. For each play Inglis gives: 1) Title; 2) Type; 3) Date. It is important for Scottish writers and their plays, especially as a number of the writers do not appear in the English catalogues.

1884 BREWER'S AUTHORS AND DATES OF DRAMAS

51 Brewer, E. Cobham. *The Reader's Handbook of Allusions, References, Plots and Stories.* 4th ed. London, Chatto and Windus 1884. 1,399 p

4,715 plays are listed. See "Authors and Dates of Dramas and Operas" p 1364–1399, which is an alphabetical listing of plays, both English and Foreign. For each play Brewer gives: 1) Title; 2) Date; 3) Surname of author; 4) Type. Dates are, at times, incorrect. Its value is negligible today. No attention should be paid to the Philadelphia edition of 1895 which lists even fewer plays.

1888 DORAN'S ANNALS OF THE ENGLISH STAGE

51A Doran, [John.] *"Their Majesties Servants." Annals Of The English Stage From Thomas Betterton to Edmund Kean.* By Dr. Doran, F.S.A. Edited and Revised By Robert W. Lowe. With Fifty Copperplate Portraits and Eighty Wood Engravings. London, John C. Nimmo, 14, King William Street, Strand MDCCCLXXXVIII. 3 vols

170 plays are listed. See Vol II Supplement to Chap XXII "List Of The Principal Dramatic Pieces Produced At The Patent Theatres, From The Retirement Of Garrick To The End Of The Eighteenth Century" 398–406. A chronological arrangement from 1776–1800.

1890 FLEAY'S CHRONICLE HISTORY

52 Fleay, Frederick Gard. *A Chronicle History of the London Stage. 1559–1642.* London, Reeves and Turner 1890. x 424 p

937 plays are listed in alphabetical order. Within its chronological limits, it is more complete than any dramatic bibliography which preceded it. In fact, the work, which has been praised and condemned by various scholars, is a mine of information and, although it must be used with caution, has been of great value to all later scholars. Of the plays listed, 565 are extant, 217 are known only from Henslowe's *Diary,* 76 are known from the *Stationers' Register;* and 27 are known from the Master of Revels entries for 1623–1624. The list is more complete "especially in second titles to plays" than Halliwell's *Dictionary* or the *Biographia Dramatica.* Today, of course, it is superseded for the most part by the works of E. K. Chambers, W. W. Greg, and G. E. Bentley.

1891 FLEAY'S BIOGRAPHICAL CHRONICLE

53 Fleay, F. G. *A Biographical Chronicle of the English Drama 1559–1642.* London, Reeves and Turner 1891. 2 vols

1,469 plays are listed and 235 authors. It is arranged alphabetically by author. The approach is that of the *Biographia Dramatica.* Within the treatment of each author the plays are listed in order of date of publication. For each play Fleay gives: 1) Date of entry in the Stationers' Register; 2) Title; 3) Type; 4) Date of first edition; 5) Remarks on the play in regard to such matters as source, staging, references to other authors. Although it is still of some value, in the main it is superseded by the work of E. K. Chambers, W. W. Greg and G. E. Bentley.

1892 HAZLITT'S MANUAL FOR THE COLLECTOR

54 Hazlitt, W. Carew. *A Manual for the Collector of Old English Plays. Edited From the Material Formed by Kirkman, Langbaine, Downes, Oldys, and Halliwell-Phillips, With Extensive Additions and Corrections.* London, Pickering & Chatto 1892. 284 p

2,369 plays are listed. The terminal date is 1700 and the arrangement is alphabetical by title of play. Based upon Halliwell's *Dictionary of Old English Plays* and influenced by Fleay's work, Hazlitt's *Manual* has additions and corrections which make it of value. In general he gives less information on individual works, however, than Halliwell. For each play he gives: 1) Title; 2) Author; 3) Theatre; 4) Format; 5) Date of publication, as well as various editions known to him; 6) Some remarks on source, resumé of plot, or merits of the play. Cross references are used. See W. C. Hazlitt, "Bibliographical and Literary Notes on the Old English Drama" *Antiquary* xx (July - Dec 1889) 14–17 60–63 106–111 198–202

1896 BATES' ENGLISH DRAMA

55 Bates, Katharine Lee, and Lydia Boker Godfrey. *English Drama.* A Working Basis. [Boston, Press of S. G. Robinson] 1896. 151 p

750 plays are listed and 233 playwrights. It is divided into chronological periods with an alphabetical arrangement by author within each division. The plays are listed in chronological order under the author's name. Critical reference works are also noted. Obviously many of the plays were never seen by the author. As a list of plays the work is most incomplete and should not be used.

1897 Evans' List of Masques

56 Evans, Herbert Arthur. *English Masques*. London, Blackie & Son, Ltd. 1898. 245 p

> 50 masques are listed. The appendix gives a "Chronological List of Masques Extant in Print, 1604–1640," which is intended to be a complete list of masques still in print. For each masque Evans gives: 1) Date of production; 2) Author; 3) Title; 4) Date and particulars of publication. Although the work had some value in its day, it is superseded by W. W. Greg's *A List of Masques* (1902).

1899 Scott's Drama of Yesterday

57 Scott, Clement. *The Drama Of Yesterday & Today*. London, Macmillan And Co.; New York, The Macmillan Company 1899. 2 vols

> 2,207 plays are listed. In the appendix of vol II the author has a "List Of Important Plays Produced In London Between 1830 (The End of Genest's History) To The Close Of The Century." For each play Scott gives: 1) Title; 2) Author; 3) Theatre; 4) Date of staging. In its own day the work was of value but today it is superseded by the Hand-Lists in Allardyce Nicoll's *History of English Drama* for the nineteenth century.

1900 Greg's List of English Plays

58 Greg, Walter Wilson. *A List of English Plays Written Before 1643 And Printed Before 1700*. London, Printed for the Bibliographical Society, By Blades, East & Blades, March, 1900, for 1899. 158 p

> 668 plays are listed and 92 authors. The list does not include works which remained in manuscript after the end of the seventeenth century nor masques, pageants, triumphs, and dialogues. The arrangement is alphabetical by author. For each author Greg gives first the collected editions, followed by the various editions of each play in chronological order. Then, for each play, he gives: 1) Title; 2) Date of publication; 3) Format; 4) Location where copies may be found in England. There are indexes of authors and of plays. Cross references are used. A scholarly work and of value, although much of it is superseded by his *A Bibliography Of The English Printed Drama To The Restoration*.

1902 Greg's List of Masques

59 Greg, Walter Wilson. *A List of Masques, Pageants, &c. Supplementary To A List of English Plays*. London, Printed for the Bibliographical Society, By Blades, East & Blades, February 1902, For 1901. xi 35 cxxxi p

> 148 masques are listed. It is arranged alphabetically by author. For each masque Greg gives: 1) Title; 2) Date of publication; 3) Location of copies, with the British Museum call numbers. He has also addenda and corrigenda to his earlier list of plays and a reprint of the lists by Rogers and Ley, Archer, and Kirkman. A scholarly work and still of some value, although it should be used with Steele's *Plays & Masques at Court* and Harbage's *Annals*.

1903 Chambers' Mediaeval Stage

60 Chambers, E. K. *The Mediaeval Stage*. Oxford, University Press 1903. 2 vols

> Appendix "W" of Vol II gives a list of the "Representations of Mediaeval Plays, according to cities, arranged in alphabetical order. Appendix "X" gives "The Texts of Mediaeval Plays and Early Tudor Interludes, to 1653." This scholarly work is still a standard reference tool and must be used by anyone working in the field of medieval drama. It has formed the basis of most subsequent investigation. See also Carl J. Stratman, *Bibliography of Medieval Drama* (1954).

1904 ADAMS' DICTIONARY OF THE DRAMA

61 Adams, W[illiam] Davenport. *A Dictionary of the Drama: A Guide to the Plays, Playwrights, Players and Playhouses of the United Kingdom and America, from the Earliest Times to the Present.* London, Chatto and Windus 1904. Vol I A-G. viii 627 p

> 3,000 plays are listed. It is done with great care and an attempt at accuracy throughout. No more volumes were published because of the death of the compiler. In alphabetical order he lists playhouses, authors, actors, theatrical managers, writers on the subject of the theatre in general, as well as plays and characters in plays. For each play he attempts to indicate the author, the date and place of the first performance, and, in some instances, the date of first publication. The work is still of some value.

1908 MARKS' ENGLISH PASTORAL DRAMA

62 Marks, Jeannette. *English Pastoral Drama From The Restoration To The Date Of The Publication Of The "Lyrical Ballads" (1660–1798).* London, Methuen and Co. [1908]. xiii [1] 228 p

> 99 plays are listed. See *English Pastoral Plays. 1660–1798*, p 179–212, where a list of the plays is given in chronological order. For each play Marks gives: 1) Title page; 2) Library where the edition can be located. A number of the works have notes attached. Manuscript plays and the location of the manuscripts are noted. The value of this particular list lies in the fact that it separates pastoral types from other plays.

1908 SCHELLING'S ELIZABETHAN DRAMA

63 Schelling, Felix E. *Elizabethan Drama, 1558–1642. A History of the Drama in England from the Accession of Queen Elizabeth to the Closing of the Theaters, to which is prefixed a Résumé of the Earlier Drama from its Beginning.* London, Archibald Constable and Co. 1908. 2 vols

> 1,723 plays are listed. In vol II p [538]–624, Schelling gives an alphabetical list of plays "and like productions written, cited or published in English between the years 1558 and 1642." For his authorities he uses the Stationers' Register, extracts from the Accounts of the Revels at Court, Henslowe's Diary, and the works of such men as Collier, Fleay, and Hazlitt. For each play he gives: 1) Title; 2) Type; 3) Author; 4) Date of publication, and/or date of production. Cross references are frequent. The list has become a basic source for later scholars — perhaps because of its easy accessibility — who have attempted to correct the errors and add to the information found in his list. For a work which supplements and completes Schelling's study see William Creizenach, "Verloren gegangene englische Dramen aus dem Zeitalter." *Shakespeare Jahrbuch* LIV (1918) 42–49. Schelling's work is, of course, superseded by that of W. W. Greg, Alfred Harbage, and G. E. Bentley.

1909 ELDREDGE'S "STAGE" CYCLOPAEDIA

64 ["Clarence, Reginald," pseud. for H. J. Eldrege.] *"The Stage" Cyclopaedia. A Bibliography of Plays. An Alphabetical List of Plays and other Stage Pieces of which any record can be found since the commencement of the English Stage, together with Descriptions, Author's Names, Dates and Places of Production, and other Useful Information, comprising in all nearly 50,000 Plays, and Extending Over a Period of Upwards of 500 Years.* London, "The Stage" 1909. 503 p

> Approximately 30,000 plays are listed. It is perhaps the most complete one volume index of plays attempted, although the author indulges in wishful thinking when he says that

he has nearly 50,000 plays. The number is closer to 30,000. Naturally, in a work of such magnitude, a good number of errors are bound to occur, especially since the author so often relies on secondary sources for his information. Both English and foreign plays are to be found in the work. For each play — the volume is arranged alphabetically by title of the play — he gives: 1) Title; 2) Type; 3) Number of acts; 4) Author; 5) Date of publication; 6) Theatre and date of acting, if known. For plays after the Restoration it is still a handy reference tool, in spite of its errors.

1911 BROOKE'S TUDOR DRAMA

65   Brooke, C. F. Tucker. *The Tudor Drama. A History Of English National Drama To The Retirement Of Shakespeare.* Boston, New York, Chicago, Dallas, San Francisco, Houghton Mifflin Company [1911]. xii [2] 461 p

307 plays are listed. An historical and critical study, from the medieval times to Shakespeare's retirement, each chapter is devoted to a specific phase of drama, such as comedy, tragedy, or the heroic play. Following each chapter is a list of plays which belong to the category or period. For each play the writer gives information relative to the staging, editions, and titles of critical studies. As the lists are selective, however, they are far from complete and should not be consulted to determine what plays were produced in the period covered. Instead, one should consult a standard work such as Harbage's *Annals.*

1914 BOAS' UNIVERSITY DRAMA

66   Boas, Frederick S. *University Drama In The Tudor Age.* Oxford, At The Clarendon Press 1914. vii [5] 414 p

108 plays are listed. See Appendix IV *A List Of University Plays,* p 385–390. For each play the writer gives: 1) Date of performance; 2) Name of the University where the play was performed; 3) Name of the College performing the play; 4) Title; 5) Author; 6) Any additional information available. Although the list has been superseded in a number of instances by the work of E. K. Chambers and Alfred Harbage, the study itself is still of value and has not been outdated.

1922 CANT'S BIBLIOGRAPHY FROM 1890 TO 1920

67   Cant, Monica. "A Bibliography Of English Drama From 1890 To 1920, Giving Separate Titles And Short Annotations," *The Library Association Record* XXIV (Feb 1922) 41–54

136 plays are listed and 60 authors. The arrangement is alphabetical by author. The plays of each author are listed in chronological order, according to date of first publication. For each play the writer gives: 1) Title; 2) Publisher; 3) Date of publication; 4) Format; 5) Pagination. As the list is a selective one, its utility is somewhat diminished. Since there is no complete list of plays for the first quarter of the twentieth century, however, it is still of some value.

1923 CHAMBERS' ELIZABETHAN STAGE

68   Chambers, E. K. *The Elizabethan Stage.* Oxford, At the Clarendon Press 1923. 4 vols

1,123 plays are listed. A standard reference work, which is still of great value today. Vol III lists 192 authors, arranged in alphabetical order, with a brief life of each dramatist, a list of collections, and the dramatist's plays arranged in chronological order of writing. Vol IV has 90 anonymous plays in alphabetical order and, in addition, a series of appendices devoted to a list of 78 lost plays, 57 manuscript plays, 56 academic plays, and 406 printed plays arranged in chronological order. This play list of printed plays is valuable and is arranged eight columns to a page. For each play, Chambers gives: 1) Date of entry in Stationers' Register; 2) Date of printing; 3) Title; 4) Name of person who entered the play in the Stationers' Register; 5) Printer; 6) Publisher; 7) Source; 8) Author. The list begins in 1557–8 and ends in 1622, although its stated limitations are 1558 and 1616. Gerald Eades Bentley's *The Jacobean and Caroline Stage* begins after 1616. Chambers' work must still be used by anyone working in the field, although it should be checked against the work of Harbage and Greg.

1924 LOGASA'S INDEX TO ONE-ACT PLAYS

69 Logasa, Hannah, and Winifred Ver Nooy. *An Index To One-Act Plays.* Boston, F. W. Faxon Company 1924. 327 p

—— Supplement, 1924–1931. Boston, F. W. Faxon Company 1932. 432 p

—— Second Supplement, 1932–1940. Boston, F. W. Faxon Company 1941. 556 p

Logasa, Hannah. *An Index To One-Act Plays for Stage and Radio. Third Supplement,* 1941–1948. Boston, F. W. Faxon Company 1950. 318 p

—— *Fourth Supplement,* 1948–1957. Boston, F. W. Faxon Company 1958. 245 p

5,000 and more one-act play titles in English or translated into English and published since 1900 are listed in the first volume. For each work the compilers give: 1) Title; 2) Author; 3) Number and kinds of characters; 4) Setting or background; 5) Suitability for elementary or high school pupils; 6) Letters which refer to the key showing the book or magazine where the play may be found.

The first supplement lists over 7,000 plays and over 500 collections; the second supplement almost 8,000 plays and over 500 collections; the third supplement about 4,000 plays. A standard reference work.

1926 STEELE'S PLAYS AND MASQUES AT COURT

70 Steele, Mary Susan. *Plays & Masques at Court During the Reigns of Elizabeth, James and Charles.* New Haven, Yale University Press; London, Humphrey Milford, Oxford University Press 1926. [6] vii–xiii [3] 300 p

379 plays are listed and 89 authors. Based primarily upon official records and contemporary allusions — sometimes at second hand — the compilation is arranged in chronological order within the period of each monarch's reign, extending from 1558 to 1642. The compilation for each reign is followed by "Miscellaneous Court Performances Of Uncertain Date." For each play Steele gives: 1) Exact date, when possible; 2) Title; 3) Name of company performing the play; 4) Payment to the actors; 5) Source of information; 6) Other sources for information; 7) Any miscellaneous facts available on the play. There are indexes of authors and of plays. Although the work is still of some use as a quick reference guide for court performances, the list of plays as well as the information on the acting companies, it should be used in conjunction with Harbage's *Annals* and Bentley's *Jacobean and Caroline Stage,* as well as Greg's *Bibliography.*

1927 FIRKINS' INDEX TO PLAYS, 1800–1926

71 Firkins, Ina Ten Eyck. *Index to Plays 1800–1926.* New York, The H. W. Wilson Company 1927. [10] 307 p

—— Supplement, *1927–1934.* New York, Wilson 1935. 140 p

7,872 plays are listed and 2,203 authors in the main volume. The index is alphabetical by author. The plays are arranged under the author's name in alphabetical order. For each play Firkins gives: 1) Title; 2) Imprint; 3) Pagination; 4) Format; 5) Type of play; 6) Number of acts. If the play appears in collections, the title of the collection is noted. Further, if the play appears in a periodical, the full information concerning the periodical is given. The index includes English and American plays as well as translations of foreign works. "The Title and Subject Index" gives the title of the play and the author. A handy quick reference guide. Of particular value for the twentieth century.

1931 GREG'S DRAMATIC DOCUMENTS

72 Greg, W. W. *Dramatic Documents From the Elizabethan Playhouses. Stage Plots: Actors' Parts: Prompt Books. Commentary.* Oxford, At the Clarendon Press 1931. xiii [1] 378 p

42 plays are listed in the *Descriptive List of Manuscript Plays* p 237–269. This is a classified list of extant manuscript plays written for production on the regular stage before the civil war closed the theatres. Thus, Greg generally excludes from the list miracles, moralities, interludes, academic plays, masques, and the like. The descriptions are still of value, although a more complete list seems to be available in Harbage's *Annals*.

1932 BOSWELL'S RESTORATION COURT STAGE

73 Boswell, Eleanore. *The Restoration Court Stage (1660–1702). With a Particular Account of The Production Of Calisto.* Cambridge, Massachusetts, Harvard University Press 1932. xviii 370 p

Appendix C gives "A Calendar Of Plays Acted at Court," in chronological order, between 1660 and 1697. For 135 of the 159 performances noted, there is documentary evidence. The author admits, however, that the list probably represents only about one-fourth of the performances at court and that much of the material is conjectural. The work is superseded by the volume of *The London Stage* devoted to the Restoration period.

1933 SIBLEY'S LOST PLAYS AND MASQUES

74 Sibley, Gertrude Marian. *The Lost Plays and Masques, 1500–1642.* Ithaca, New York, Cornell University Press 1933. xii [2] 205 p

870 titles of plays and masques are listed. The first list is of plays from 1558 to 1642, arranged in alphabetical order. In this section the writer attempts to bring all known information together. The material on plays written between 1500 and 1558 is naturally less complete. The second list is devoted to masques and the titles are arranged in alphabetical order. For each entry Sibley attempts to bring together all contemporary references to each work; next she summarizes opinions of scholars as to the nature of the plots. It is still of value today, especially, as a quick guide to the lost plays and masques. Part of the material is superseded by Gerald E. Bentley's *Jacobean and Caroline Stage*, especially in regard to critical commentary. Further, the basic list itself is also, in a sense, superseded by Harbage's *Annals*.

1934 BARRETT'S CHART OF PLAYS

75 Barrett, W. P., compiler. *Chart of Plays, 1584 to 1623.* Cambridge, At the University Press 1934. 39 p

408 plays are listed in chronological order, with three columns to each page and fifteen columns devoted to each date. The columns are arranged as follows: 1) Political and social events in the year; 2) Literary and theatrical events in the year; 3) Shakespeare activity; 4–13) Individual authors; 14) Masks and plays by minor dramatic writers; 15) Anonymous plays and masques. As a chronological arrangement of the plays the *Chart* is, of course, superseded by Harbage's *Annals*. As a handbook or annals of literary activity for the period it is of questionable value.

[1934] SUMMERS' RESTORATION DRAMA

76 Summers, Montague. *A Bibliography of the Restoration Drama.* London, The Fortune Press [1934]. 143 p

790 plays are listed and 169 authors. 86 of the plays are anonymous. The arrangement is alphabetical by author, with the plays listed under the author's name in chronological order. For each play, Summers gives: 1) Title; 2) Type; 3) Whether acted; 4) Theatre; 5) Date of acting; 6) Format; 7) Date of first edition; 8) Subsequent editions. There are a number of errors relative to date of acting, theatre, and dates of individual editions. As far as titles and dates it is superseded by Allardyce Nicoll's work on the Restoration drama, which includes the "Hand-List" of plays. Further, in relation to information concerning the actual staging of the plays, it is superseded by the volume of *The London Stage* devoted to the Restoration.

1936 HARBAGE'S CAVALIER DRAMA

77 Harbage, Alfred. *Cavalier Drama. An Historical and Critical Supplement To the Study of the Elizabethan and Restoration Stage.* New York, Modern Language Association of America; London, Oxford University Press 1936. 302 p

663 plays are listed in "A List, Chronologically Arranged of All Plays of the Caroline, Commonwealth, and Early Restoration Periods [1626–1668]," p 259–285. The list is based upon the standard sources. For each play the author gives: 1) Author; 2) Title; 3) Type; 4) Professional company producing the play; 5) Date of earliest publication. This play list is, of course, superseded by the author's own *Annals*, which carries the work to 1700.

1937 McCABE'S PLAY-LIST OF ST OMERS

78 McCabe, William H. "The Play-List of The English College of St Omers. 1592–1762." *Revue de Littérature Comparée*, xvii (1937) 355–375

Several dozen Latin plays are listed in chronological order from the founding of the school in 1592 to the closing in 1762, when Jesuit property was seized in France. The play list is not complete, but for each play McCabe gives: 1) Title; 2) Author; 3) Date of production; 4) Brief outline of the plot. The reason for including the list in the present survey is that the college was thoroughly English and fostered an active dramatic spirit and that some of the manuscripts found their way back to England.

1938 MacMILLAN'S DRURY-LANE CALENDAR

79 MacMillan, Dougald. *Drury-Lane Calendar, 1747–1776. Compiled from the Playbills And Edited With an Introduction.* Published in Co-operation with the Huntington Library. Oxford, At the Clarendon Press 1938. xxiii 364 p

383 plays are listed. It is based upon the Kemble-Devonshire collection of Drury Lane Playbills in the Huntington Library and completed from the files of the *General Advertiser* and its successor, *The Public Advertiser*. The calendar of performances at Drury Lane begins on September 15 1747 and ends on June 10 1776. Part I consists of the calendar of performances and Part II of an "Alphabetical List of Plays" p 202–347. In this list MacMillan gives for each play: 1) Dates of performance; 2) Cast; 3) Author. Naturally, revivals are included in the listing. It is superseded by *The London Stage, 1747–1776,* edited and compiled by George Winchester Stone, Jr.

1939 MacMILLAN'S LARPENT PLAYS

80 MacMillan, Dougald, comp. *Catalogue of the Larpent Plays in the Huntington Library.* San Marino, California [n.p.] 1939. xv [1] 442 p

2,502 numbered entries for plays are listed. It is arranged chronologically beginning in 1737 and ending in 1823. There are indexes of authors and of plays. For each entry MacMillan gives: 1) The title as it appears on the manuscript; 2) Type; 3) Author, when known; 4) Date of application for license; 5) Name of the theatre manager; 6) Theatre; 7) Date of the first production; 8) A statement as to whether the copy is in manuscript form or is printed; 9) Noteworthy peculiarities of the copy; 10) Compares the manuscript or manuscripts with the printed text to note the differences. In all, it is an excellent catalogue and should be consulted by anyone working in the field. See also the following articles: 1) Louis Francis Peck, "M. G. Lewis and the Larpent Catalogue" *Huntington Library Quarterly* v (1941–42) 382–384. This article indicates that six Larpent manuscripts which are included in the *Catalogue,* without attribution, should be added to the works of M. G. Lewis. 2) Ethel Pearce, "The Larpent Plays, Additions and Corrections" *Huntington Library Quarterly* vi (1943) 491–494.

1939 Greg's Bibliography of English Printed Drama

81 Greg, W. W. *A Bibliography Of The English Printed Drama To The Restoration.* London, Printed For The Bibliographical Society At The University Press, Oxford 1939–1959. 4 vols

1,023 plays are listed. Vols I and II contain 836 plays numbered consecutively and arranged in chronological order. 811 of the 836 plays were printed between 1512 and 1659. Vol II has twenty-six Latin plays dated from 1581 to 1658, and in addition, lists the titles of 187 lost plays dated from 1504 to 1662. Vol III notes the various collections of plays in alphabetical order by author from 1604 to 1661. Finally, Vol IV has additions and corrections to the first two vols. For each play in vols I and II, Greg gives: 1) Date of writing; 2) Stationers' Register entry; 3) Full title page; 4) Notice of any variant imprints; 5) Running title; 6) Colophon, if any; 7) Collation; 8) Catchwords; 9) Form the play was written in; 10) Notes on peculiarities, in regard to copies in specific libraries; 11) Various editions of a play are given, with the same information. Only the name of the author is omitted, if it does not appear on the title page. A model of bibliographical information, it is the standard reference work for the period.

1940 Harbage's Annals of English Drama

82 Harbage, Alfred. *Annals of English Drama, 975–1700. An Analytical Record of All Plays, Extant or Lost, Chronologically Arranged And Indexed by Authors, Titles, Dramatic Companies, etc.* Philadelphia, University of Pennsylvania Press 1940. 264 p

3,351 plays are listed and 680 authors. The basic division is a chronological listing of plays from 975 to 1700. In this section seven columns are devoted to information about each of the plays and the information given in each column is as follows: 1) Author; 2) Title; 3) Historical limits; 4) Type; 5) Auspices of the first production; 6) Date of the first edition; 7) Date of the last edition. Harbage's work also contains two supplementary lists: 1) Extant plays omitted from the chronological listing because of their uncertain date and identity; 2) Non-extant plays omitted from the chronology because of their uncertain date and identity. Finally, it has the following indexes: 1) English Playwrights; 2) English Plays; 3) Foreign Playwrights; 4) Foreign Plays translated or adapted; 5) Dramatic Companies. An appendix gives a list of extant play manuscripts from 975 to 1700, wherein are noted 404 manuscript plays, 258 with authors, and 146 anonymous. An excellent work and the most handy one volume reference work for plays before 1700. Errors and omissions have been corrected by Samuel Schoenbaum in the revised edition, published in 1964.

See the following articles by Alfred Harbage: 1) "Elizabethan and Seventeenth-Century Play Manuscripts" *PMLA* l (1935) 687–699. He locates 248 manuscripts. This material is included in the *Annals.* 2) "Elizabethan and Seventeenth-Century Play Manuscripts: Addenda" *PMLA* lii (1937) 905–907. 26 manuscripts are added to the 1935 list and also included in the *Annals.* 3) "A Census of Anglo-Latin Plays" *PMLA* liii (1938) 624–629. 135 Anglo-Latin plays written in England or by Englishmen abroad during the sixteenth and seventeenth centuries are listed. This material is also included in the *Annals.*

1940 Wells' List of Extant Plays

83 Wells, Henry W. *A Chronological List of Extant Plays Produced In Or About London 1581–1642.* Prepared by Henry W. Wells As a Supplement To His

Elizabethan and Jacobean Playwrights. New York, Columbia University Press 1940. 17 p

482 plays are listed. It gives each play under the year in which it is "either known to have been produced or most likely to have been produced." School and closet dramas, as well as masques and translations, are not included. For each play Wells gives: 1) Title; 2) Author; 3) Date of publication. Although the standard sources were used in gathering the material, it has little value today, especially in view of Greg's *Bibliography* and Harbage's *Annals.*

1941 CAMBRIDGE BIBLIOGRAPHY OF ENGLISH LITERATURE

84 *The Cambridge Bibliography Of English Literature.* Edited by F. W. Bateson. New York, The Macmillan Company; Cambridge, England, At The University Press 1941. 4 vols

3,473 plays are listed and 519 authors. In the various sections devoted to the drama, some 519 authors are listed, with 3,268 plays attributed to them. Some 205 plays are listed before the Restoration as anonymous, but after the Restoration there is no attempt to list anonymous plays. Further, with a few notable exceptions, no playwright of the nineteenth century has more than eight plays listed after his name. For the other plays by a specific playwright the reader is told to consult Allardyce Nicoll's "Hand-List." A good many playwrights, as well as a large number of plays, are omitted. As the work on the various sections was contributed by different compilers, there is a great unevenness. In fact, rather than this *Bibliography,* one should use Nicoll's hand-lists or, for various specific periods, the standard tools by E. K. Chambers, W. W. Greg, Alfred Harbage, and Gerald E. Bentley.

1941 BENTLEY's JACOBEAN AND CAROLINE STAGE

85 Bentley, Gerald Eades. *The Jacobean and Caroline Stage.* Oxford, At the Clarendon Press 1941–56. 5 vols

842 plays are listed and 208 authors. 267 of the plays are anonymous. See vols III through V, which study the plays and playwrights. Under the word "plays" Bentley includes all masques, shows, and dramatic entertainments. His treatment is limited to the works written or first performed in England between 1616 and 1642, with a few exceptions which extend the date limitations in both directions. The playwrights are arranged in alphabetical order and the plays for each author appear in alphabetical order under his name. For each author Bentley gives: 1) Bibliography; 2) Biography; 3) Collected editions in chronological order; 4) Discussion of individual plays in alphabetical order, based upon the latest research. For each play he gives: 1) The manuscript title and location, if known; 2) Bibliography of the play and what scholars say of it; 3) Stationers' Register entry or contemporary document reference; 4) Various editions; 5) Discussion of all known information about the play, for Bentley has brought together all the latest scholarship on each of the writers and plays. A scholarly and standard reference work, it must be used by anyone working in the period.

1945 WOODWARD AND McMANAWAY's CHECK LIST

86 Woodward, Gertrude L., and James G. McManaway. *A Check List of English Plays, 1641–1700.* Chicago, The Newberry Library 1945 [10] 155 p

1,340 numbered entries list 758 plays and 222 authors. Sixty-nine of the plays are anonymous. The arrangement is alphabetical by author, with anonymous works fitted into the alphabetical grouping. A supplement gives corrections and additions. The *Check List* records the plays and masques with the variant editions and issues printed in the English language in the British Isles or in other countries, from 1641 to 1700. Short titles are used for each of the plays. For each play the compilers give: 1) Title; 2) Printer; 3) Date of edition; 4) Format; 5) Libraries in the United States which possess a copy. It is still satisfactory as a quick reference guide. For additions and corrections, however, see

Fredson Bowers, *A Supplement to the Woodward and McManaway Check List of English Plays, 1641–1700* (Charlottesville, Bibliographical Society of the Univ of Virginia 1949. 22 p Mimeographed)

1946 Thomson's Index to Full Length Plays

87 Thomson, Ruth Gibbons. *Index To Full Length Plays, 1926–1944.* Boston, The F. W. Faxon Company 1946. ix [1] 306 p

1,340 plays are listed and 879 authors. The *Index* is a selection of full-length plays published in English during the years 1926 to 1944 in England and the United States. The main entry is by title of the play. For each entry Thomson gives: 1) Title; 2) Author or translator; 3) Number of acts; 4) Characters; 5) Sets; 6) Subject matter. The title index is followed by an author and subject index which has 572 subject headings. The plays included in this *Index* were published and successfully produced in England and the United States. An asterisk is employed to indicate non-royalty plays. It is of value if one remembers that it is a selective and not a complete list of plays for the period.

1950 The Player's Library

88 *The Player's Library.* The Catalogue of the Library of the British Drama League. With an Introduction by Frederick S. Boas. [London] Published For The British Drama League by Faber and Faber Limited [1950]. xvi [2] 1115 p

—— *First Supplement To The Player's Library.* The Catalogue of the Library of the British Drama League. [London] Published for The British Drama League by Faber and Faber Limited [1951]. 128 p

—— *Second Supplement To The Player's Library. . . .* Published for the British Drama League by Faber and Faber Limited [1954] 256 p

—— *Third Supplement To The Player's Library. . . .* Published for the British Drama League by Faber and Faber Limited [1956]. 256 p

At least 14,500 plays are listed in the main volume, which has a title index of plays. The collection concentrates mostly on acting editions. Although the list is basically for English works, American plays appear as well as translations from the Russian, French, German, and Italian. As the work is an author catalogue of plays, for each play it gives: 1) Number of acts; 2) Cast; 3) Setting; 4) Period and costume; 5) Publisher's name. Such facts as date of publication, pagination, and editions are generally not given.

The first supplement has approximately 1,600 play titles, the second approximately 3,200, and the third approximately 2,000. Of course, the main value of the work lies in the total number of plays listed and the fact that they are to be found in The Player's Library in London; the dating, however, is weak.

1951 Ottemiller's Index to Plays in Collections

89 Ottemiller, John H. *Index to Plays in Collections. An author and title index to plays appearing in collections published between 1900 and 1950.* Second Edition, Revised and Enlarged. Washington, D.C., The Scarecrow Press 1951. x 11–386 p

4,933 plays are listed and 948 authors from the Greek to the present day. It is limited to books published in England and the United States, although plays in foreign languages, which are published in anthologies, are included. Only complete texts of standard full length plays are noted. Thus, children's plays, amateur, one act, radio or television plays are not indexed. It is divided into: 1) Author's Index, which gives the author's name and dates, the title of the play, and the date of the first production, together with the symbols for the Collection or Collections in which the play is located; 2) A List of Collections Analyzed is arranged alphabetically by symbols, wherein the symbol is followed by the compiler's name, the title of the collection, the imprint, pagination, and list of plays in the volume arranged alphabetically by author; 3) A Title Index, with the title of the play followed by the name of the author.

A standard reference work, the first edition of the *Index* appeared in 1943. A third revised edition appeared in 1957 and a fourth in 1964 which indexed 6,993 copies of 2,536 different plays by 1,300 authors and analyzed 814 Collections.

1951 WHITE'S RISE OF ENGLISH OPERA

90 White, Eric Walter. *The Rise Of English Opera.* With An Introduction by Benjamin Britten. London, John Lehmann 1951. 335 p

589 operas are listed from 1590 to 1951. See Appendix A "A Short List of English Operas and Semi-Operas and their First Performances" p 213–274. For each opera which is listed under its title in chronological order, White gives: 1) Title; 2) Date of production; 3) Place and theatre; 4) Composer; 5) Librettist; 6) Number of acts. This is the standard reference work for English opera. See also White's article "A Decade Of English Opera, 1951–60" *Theatre Notebook* xv (Summer 1961) 110–115, which lists an additional 57 English operas.

1952 NICOLL'S HISTORY OF ENGLISH DRAMA

91 Nicoll, Allardyce. *A History of English Drama, 1660–1900.* Cambridge, Cambridge Univ Press 1952–1959. 6 vols rev eds

Vol I *Restoration Drama, 1660–1700* (4th ed 1952; 1st ed 1923); Vol II *Early Eighteenth Century, 1700–1750* (3rd ed 1952; 1st ed 1925); Vol III *Late Eighteenth Century Drama, 1750–1800* (2nd ed 1952; 1st ed 1927); Vol IV *Early Nineteenth Century Drama, 1800–1850* (2nd ed 1955; 1st ed 1930); Vol V *Late Nineteenth Century Drama, 1850–1900* (2nd ed 1959; 1st ed 1946) Vol VI *A Short-Title Alphabetical Catalogue of Plays* (1959)

Approximately 25,000 works such as plays, operas, and masques are listed. In the second section of each volume is a "Hand-List of Plays" arranged by author in alphabetical order. Each play is placed in chronological order under a specific author's name and for each one Nicoll gives: 1) Title; 2) Type; 3) Date of the first and subsequent editions; 4) Dates of production; 5) Theatre. Following the list of authors are the plays by unknown authors arranged in alphabetical order. Next is a list of Italian Operas and Oratorios. Each volume has a supplementary section which gives additional material located since the publication of the first edition. The index volume has copious cross references as well as additional corrections concerning dates or attribution.

Nicoll's work represents the most complete attempt to bring together all the English works from 1660 to 1900. There are, of course, a number of errors and omissions in it, as it is a practical impossibility for one man to control such a large number of entries without errors creeping in. For additions and corrections, some of which were incorporated in Nicoll's later editions, see the following articles:

a) Rhodes, R. Crompton. "The Early Nineteenth-Century Drama" *The Library* 4th Ser xvi (1935) 91–112 210–231. The writer notes plays between 1800 and 1850 not in Nicoll and also indicates some dates which are incorrect in Nicoll's "Hand-List."

b) Wood, Frederick Thomas. "Unrecorded xviii Century Plays" *Notes and Queries* clxx (1936) 56–58 319; clxxii (1938) 188. The writer gives 104 titles drawn from various collections of provincial playbills and newspapers of the eighteenth century. Most are short after-pieces.

c) Babcock, R. W. "Eighteenth-Century Comic Opera Manuscripts" *PMLA* lii (1937) 907–908. A list of twelve comic opera manuscripts, British Museum Catalogue 91 of Dramatic Manuscripts.

d) Miller, Frances Schouler. "Notes on Some Eighteenth Century Dramas" *Modern Language Notes* lii (March 1937) 203–206. The article contains additions and corrections to Nicoll's "Hand-List," as well as the titles of several plays not listed by Nicoll.

e) Biella, A. "Additions and Corrections to the Bibliography of Nineteenth-Century British Drama" *Philological Quarterly* xxi (July 1942) 298–322. For 1800–1850, Biella gives forty-one plays and authors not in Nicoll; 58 composers not listed in Nicoll as identified; and 81 sources, translations, adaptations, and parallels unnoted in Nicoll's work. He also identifies 63 plays not known to Nicoll.

f) Ewing, Majl. "The Authorship of Some Nineteenth-Century Plays" *Modern Language Notes* lvii (June 1942) 466–468. The writer identifies fifteen plays not listed in Nicoll for 1800–1850.

g) Ewing, Majl. "Notes on Nicoll's Handlist for 1800–1850" *Modern Language Notes* lviii (June 1943) 460–464. He gives the correct attribution for a number of plays incorrectly listed by Nicoll.

h) Tobin, James Edward. "More English Plays: 1800–1850." *Philological Quarterly* xxiii (Oct 1944) 320–332. He adds to Nicoll's "Hand-List" some 67 English plays and operas with their authors and 16 plays by unknown authors.

i) Wade, Allan. "Early XIXth Century Plays" *Theatre Notebook* i (April 1946) 27–32; (July 1946) 42–43. He supplies authors' names for some 290 plays in Nicoll's "Hand-List."

j) Troubridge, St. V. "Late Eighteenth-Century Plays" *Theatre Notebook* i (April 1947) 96. He lists 14 plays not in Nicoll's "Hand-List."

k) Troubridge, St. Vincent, and Allan Wade. "Early XIXth Century Plays" *Theatre Notebook* ii (July-Sept 1948) 13–17 31–33 56–59 76–80; iv (Oct 1949) 24; (Jan-Mar 1950) 40–43; (April-June 1950) 68–71; (July-Sept 1950) 81–84. He lists hundreds of corrections and additions of plays to Nicoll's "Hand-List."

1) Stratman, Carl J., C.S.V. "Additions to Allardyce Nicoll's Hand-List of Plays: 1800–1818" *Notes and Queries* New Ser viii (June 1961) 214–217. He lists 11 tragedies not in Nicoll. In all 38 additions or changes are given.

m) Stratman, Carl J., C.S.V. "English Tragedy: 1819–1823" *Philological Quarterly* xli (April 1962) 465–474. He lists 10 tragedies which are not in Nicoll. In all 35 additions are given.

1953 Play Index of West and Peake

92 West, Dorothy Herbert, and Dorothy Margaret Peake, comps. *Play Index, 1949–1952. An Index To 2,616 Plays In 1,138 Volumes.* New York, The H. W. Wilson Company 1953. [10] 239 p

These 2,616 plays in the English language and published in the United States, England and Canada are indexed and analyzed by subject as well as author and title. It augments Firkins' work. It has plays for children and adults, in collections and single, one-act and full length, radio and television. Part I in one alphabet gives author, title and subject entries for all the plays indexed. For single plays the compilers give: 1) Title; 2) Publisher; 3) Date; 4) Pagination; 5) Type; 6) Number of acts and scenes; 7) Size of cast; 8) Number of sets. Part II lists 162 Collections; Part III gives a cast analysis; and Part IV provides a directory of publishers.

In 1963, a supplement covering the years 1953–1960 was published by Estelle A. Fidell and Dorothy Margaret Peake. The supplement is an index of 4,592 plays in 1,735 volumes and follows, with a few minor exceptions, the policies and principles used in the 1949–1952 volume. The work is of value for the years which it covers.

1954 Stratman's Bibliography of Medieval Drama

93 Stratman, Carl J., C.S.V. *Bibliography of Medieval Drama.* Berkeley and Los Angeles, Univ of California Press 1954. x 423 p

The 3,771 numbered entries are devoted to English, French, German, Italian, Latin, and Spanish medieval drama. The main body of the work is devoted to the English drama and gives not only the individual plays as well as the Cycle productions but also the titles of critical studies which deal with all phases of medieval English drama. As the actual total number of medieval English plays is relatively small, the greater part of the bibliography is devoted to the critical studies. Whenever possible, manuscripts are located. Library locations are also given for every book listed in the bibliography. An author and subject index is included.

1955 LOEWENBERG'S ANNALS OF OPERA

94 Loewenberg, Alfred. *Annals Of Opera, 1597–1940.* Compiled From The Original Sources By Alfred Loewenberg. By Edward J. Dent. Second edition, revised and corrected. Genève, Societas Bibliographica [1955]. 2 vols

Approximately 4,000 operas are listed. Although English ballad operas are included, it contains the operas of various countries. The arrangement is chronological in order of first appearance of the work on the stage. Thus, for each work Loewenberg gives: 1) Date; 2) Name of town in which the performance took place; 3) Author; 4) Literary source; 5) Translations, adaptations and revivals; 6) First edition and subsequent ones. Although this is a valuable work, anyone interested in the English opera should consult Eric Walter White's *The Rise Of English Opera* (1951).

1956 THOMSON'S INDEX TO FULL LENGTH PLAYS

95 Thomson, Ruth Gibbons. *Index To Full Length Plays, 1895 to 1925.* Boston, The F. W. Faxon Company 1956. xi 172 p

562 titles are listed in the main entry. 348 subjects have been assigned and 360 authors represented. There are three indexes, one of plays, one of authors, and one of subjects, as well as a bibliography and a list of prize plays. The arrangement is the same as in her *Index To Full Length Plays, 1926–1944* (1946).

1960 AVERY'S LONDON STAGE . . . 1700–1729

96 Avery, Emmett L. *The London Stage, 1660–1800. A Calendar of Plays, Entertainments & Afterpieces. Together with Casts, Box Receipts and Contemporary Comment. . . . Part 2: 1700–1729.* Carbondale, Southern Illinois Univ Press 1960. 2 vols

1,161 plays are listed and 164 authors. It forms a calendar of the daily entertainment at the London theatres for 1700–1729. For each entry of the performance of a play Avery gives: 1) Date; 2) Title; 3) Casts; 4) Comments, usually from a contemporary source. Although this is a calendar of performances, rather than a list of plays, it is one of the most valuable works for the years covered and must be consulted by anyone working in this period. The index in each volume lists the titles of the various plays staged. The plays listed include not only new pieces but revivals of Shakespeare, Elizabethan, and Restoration works, together with plays by foreign authors either in translation or in the original.

1961 SCOUTEN'S LONDON STAGE . . . 1729–1747

97 Scouten, Arthur H. *The London Stage, 1660–1800. A Calendar of Plays, Entertainments & Afterpieces. Together with Casts, Box Receipts and Contemporary Comments. . . . Part 3: 1729–1747.* Carbondale, Southern Illinois Univ Press 1961. 2 vols

817 plays are listed and 204 authors. It forms a calendar of the daily entertainment at the London theatres for 1729–1747. For each entry of the performance of a play, Scouten gives: 1) Date; 2) Title; 3) Casts; 4) Comments, usually from a contemporary source. Although this is a calendar of performances, rather than a list of plays, it is one of the

most valuable works for the years covered and must be consulted by anyone working in this period. The index in each volume lists the titles of the various plays staged. The plays listed include not only new pieces but revivals of Shakespeare, Elizabethan, Restoration works, earlier eighteenth century titles, together with plays by foreign authors either in translation or the original.

1962   STONE'S LONDON STAGE . . . 1747–1776

98   Stone, George Winchester, Jr. *The London Stage, 1660–1800. A Calendar of Plays, Entertainments & Afterpieces. Together with Casts, Box Receipts and Contemporary Comment. . . . Part 4: 1747–1776.*   Carbondale, Southern Illinois University Press 1962. 3 vols

985 plays are listed and 255 authors. It forms a calendar of the daily entertainment at the London theatres for 1747–1776. For each entry of the performance of a play, Stone gives: 1) Date; 2) Title; 3) Casts; 4) Comments, usually from a contemporary source. Although this is a calendar of performances, rather than a list of plays, it is one of the most valuable works for the years covered and must be consulted by anyone working in this period. The index in each volume lists the titles of the various plays staged. The plays listed include not only new pieces but revivals of Shakespeare, Elizabethan, Restoration works, earlier 18th Century titles, together with plays by foreign authors either in translation or in the original.

1963   BERGQUIST'S CHECKLIST

99   Bergquist, G. William, ed.   *Three Centuries Of English And American Plays: A Checklist. England: 1500–1800. United States: 1714–1830.*   New York and London, Hafner Publishing Company 1963. xii 281 p

Approximately 5,500 plays are listed as well as 1,000 English and 162 American authors. Although the compiler calls the work a "Checklist," it is basically an index of the Microprint edition of *Three Centuries of English and American Plays.* The reason for calling it an index rather than a checklist is simply because the compiler or editor limits his entries to those that are to be found in the microprint edition, thus omitting several hundred plays not to be found in microprint. As an index it is well done. Arranged under one alphabet are authors and titles of anonymous plays. For each author Bergquist gives: 1) The author's full name; 2) Birth and death dates; 3) A list of the author's plays in alphabetical order. For each play he gives: 1) Title; 2) Imprint; 3) Section of the microprint where the play will be found; 4) When applicable, the Greg, the Woodward and McManaway, and the Frank P. Hill entry numbers for American plays. Cross references appear a number of times.

Index
(by entry number)